BIRTH OF A BALLET

Birth of a Ballet

by

Richard Austin

Line drawings by Judy Ling Wong
Photographs by Alan Cunliffe
with a foreword by Christopher Bruce

VISION

792·82

Vision Press Limited
11-14 Stanhope Mews West
London SW7 5RD

ISBN 0 85478 044 0

7702

CHY — CS

Printed in Great Britain
by Clarke, Doble & Brendon Ltd., Plymouth
MCMLXXVI

For Christopher Bruce and his dancers

Dancer, O you who are the postponement
of all that fades in eternal flow: how you give us yourself.
And then the final whirl, this tree growing out of movement,
did it not take total possession of the accomplished year?

Rainer Maria Rilke

Sonnets to Orpheus

Contents

Acknowledgements

In the first instance I should like to thank the Directors of Ballet Rambert and the Mercury Theatre Trust Ltd for kindly allowing me facilities to study the ballet *Black Angels*. I am particularly indebted to Mr Christopher Bruce, Associate Director of the Company, for the opportunity to watch him at work on the ballet. I should also like to thank the following dancers of Ballet Rambert who agreed to this and for the consideration they showed to me—Miss Catherine Becque, Miss Lucy Burge, Miss Sylvia Yamada, Mr Zoltan Imre, Mr Bob Smith and Mr Leigh Warren. I am most grateful to Miss Nadine Baylis who, despite a very crowded schedule, set aside time to discuss her designs. I am very grateful to Mr John B. Read who kindly allowed me to discuss lighting design with him at very short notice on the day of the first performance of *Black Angels*. I should also like to thank Miss Valerie Bourne and Miss Seona Reid, Public Relations and Press Officers of Ballet Rambert, for their help in many ways. I must also thank Miss Mary Scudamore who helped me to correct the typescript and proofs. For much of the background material relating to the early history of Ballet Rambert I am indebted to Mary Clarke's *Dancers of Mercury* (1962) and the late Lionel Bradley's *Sixteen Years of Ballet Rambert* (1946).

For permission to use copyright material, acknowledgements are made as follows: for quotations from *The Waste Land*, *Ash Wednesday*, *The Dry Salvages*, *Little Gidding* and *East Coker* from *Collected Poems 1909–1962* by T. S. Eliot, and from "The Annunciation" taken from *The Collected Poems of Edwin Muir*, both by permission of Faber and Faber Ltd; for quotations from *Duino Elegies* and *Sonnets to Orpheus* by R. M. Rilke, translated

9

Acknowledgements

by Stephen Spender and J. B. Leishman, to St John's College, Oxford and The Hogarth Press; from *The Collected Poems of Wilfred Owen* edited by C. Day Lewis, to the Estate of Wilfred Owen and Chatto and Windus Ltd; from "Easter Duties" by Elizabeth Jennings, taken from *Growing-Points*, to Carcanet Press Ltd; for "La Luna Asoma" from *Selected Poems* by García Lorca, by permission of New Directions Publishing Corporation, New York; for a quotation from *Pietà* by R. S. Thomas by permission of Rupert Hart-Davis Ltd and Granada Publishing Ltd; for quotations from "For the Nativity" and "The Last Watch of Empire" from *Selected Poems* of John Heath-Stubbs, published by Oxford University Press, by permission of David Higham Associates Ltd.

The art work, showing the dancers at rehearsals of *Black Angels*, was designed specially for this book by Judy Ling Wong. The original sketches may be purchased from the artist through the Woodstock Gallery, 16 Woodstock Street, London W.1 to whom all inquiries should be made.

Foreword

by CHRISTOPHER BRUCE

Richard Austin first wrote to me early in 1975, asking if he could write a book describing the creation of my next ballet. The idea interested me, but at the same time I was worried that there might be difficulty in achieving a totally honest account of the creative process. Under scrutiny, people are apt to behave abnormally, and I believe for a successful creation the choreographer requires a quiet studio where he and his cast can work undisturbed with complete concentration.

At the time I received his letter I was about to embark on the choreography of *Ancient Voices of Children*. I felt that the ballet would need very delicate handling, as I hoped to create something that relied on sparse and simple movement, with a reliance on a quality of stillness to convey the atmosphere I wanted. After considering Austin's idea for some time, I decided against it for the time being, but promised him that I would think about it at a later date.

As I began to plan *Black Angels*, I received another letter from Austin. It was obvious that he passionately wanted to write this book and was not going to give up the idea easily. I admired his persistence, and so we decided to give it a try and see how the first few days of rehearsals went.

I need not have worried about him intruding, for he slipped in and out of the studio as silently as a mouse, often without me noticing him at all. In fact, after a few days it occurred to me that I had been so engrossed in the ballet that I was ignoring him almost to the point of rudeness, but decided that this was probably best as it would leave him the freedom to be as objective as possible, and me the freedom to carry on as normal. As far as the cast was concerned, they worked magnificently and seemed entirely unconcerned by his presence.

11

After a week's work, I was shown the first few pages of his manuscript, and all my fears were dispelled. I was thrilled to read what he had seen in the work, and although his interpretation is a personal one and not necessarily the definitive version, if such a thing exists, I only hoped that audiences would see half as much in the ballet, and enjoy it as much as he evidently did. He threw himself into the work with marvellous energy, taking an interest in all the elements that go towards producing a ballet. He has had the freedom to write what he wished and has managed to maintain his independence to the degree that I can honestly say that I do not properly know the man, except through his work, and I think he would say the same of me.

The creation of my ballets have been amongst the most exciting times of my life. It is wonderful for me to have some of these moments captured on paper, and I would like to take this opportunity of thanking Richard Austin for his interest and passion, which have caused him to write his beautiful descriptions of those long hard hours in the studio. Also my thanks to Judy Ling Wong for her stunning drawings which capture so perfectly the despairing flight of my Black Angels.

August 1976

1. The Company

On 15th June, 1926, a small ballet by an unknown young man, Frederick Ashton, was presented by Nigel Playfair in his review, *Riverside Nights*, at the Lyric Theatre, Hammersmith. The ballet was called *A Tragedy of Fashion* in which the leading dancers were the choreographer and Marie Rambert. Fifty years later, on the same date, a gala performance was given at Sadler's Wells Theatre to celebrate the fifty years of **Ballet Rambert**. The leading dancer of *A Tragedy of Fashion*, the founder-director and guiding genius of the Company, was on the stage to meet her acclaim. Somehow Ballet Rambert has survived, despite so many financial crises, the loss of so many dancers, and the lack of a permanent home.

Marie Rambert was born in Warsaw in 1888. Her mother was of Russian origin and her father a citizen of Warsaw, then under Russian domination. She showed while at school a precocious aptitude for the dance, and this was reinforced by her first sight of Isadora Duncan whose art was to become the central inspiration of her life. In 1905 she went to Paris, originally to study medicine, but she soon became involved in the city's intellectual and artistic life. She began to give her own dance recitals in Paris salons, where her vivid personality and her sense of total involvement in the dance were recognized by Raymond Duncan, Isadora's brother, thus forming another link with her muse.

In 1910 she went to the Dalcroze School of Eurhythmics in Geneva, studying there for three years. It was through her work with Dalcroze that she first became acquainted with Serge Diaghilev, and in 1912 she joined his company to teach eurhythmics and to help Nijinsky, who had no musical training, to unravel Stravinsky's complex score for *The Rite of Spring* for which he was composing the choreography. She remained in the company for two years, dancing in the *corps de ballet* and giving her classes in eurhythmics to somewhat unenthusiastic dancers who felt that their background at the Imperial School of Russian Ballet had given them everything they could possibly need.

Dame Marie's devotion to the classical dance was partly influenced by the art of Anna Pavlova, to whom she gave the same reverence as she did to Isadora Duncan, but mainly by a period of study with Enrico Cecchetti, the great maestro of classicism, in London where she had settled in 1914. Married to the distinguished playwright Ashley Dukes in 1918, she then opened her own school of dancing at Notting Hill. It is from that moment that the history of ballet in this country can truly be said to begin. If it had not been for Dame Marie Rambert it would certainly be different, not so rich, so rapid in growth, or so profoundly influential throughout Europe and America. If the art of Isadora Duncan was her inheritance, the existence of ballet in this country is her bequest.

For the four years from 1926 until 1930 Marie Rambert arranged small ballets for her students. In 1930 she presented a ballet matinée, again at the Lyric Theatre, Hammersmith, at which Frederick Ashton's ballet, *Capriol Suite*, to the music of Peter Warlock was presented, and her pupils were, for the first time, recognized as a true ballet company. This led to a fortnight's season, at which the great Karsavina appeared, teaching the Company *Les Sylphides* as she had been taught it by Fokine himself.

It was due to Marie Rambert's extraordinary enthusiasm and the sense of dedication existing within her small Company that it not only began to develop remarkable dancers of its own, such as Harold Turner, Pearl Argyle and Diana Gould, but also attracted great artists from the Diaghilev era. Karsavina was followed by Leon Woizikowski and later Alicia Markova—the last of Diaghilev's ballerinas, too young, alas, to dance many leading roles in his Company before his death. The studio at Notting Hill Gate was converted into the Mercury Theatre, and visited by Anna Pavlova a year before her death, thus giving to the new Company a treasured link with the past and with the greatest of all classical ballerinas. The Ballet Club was then formed, and gave its first performance on 11th February, 1931.

The Ballet Club continued to exist until 1939, during which time Ballet Rambert became accepted by a far wider public than those who had first visited the Mercury Theatre. In 1931, at a performance arranged by the Camargo Society using the Rambert dancers, Frederick Ashton's ballet, *Façade*, with the great Diaghilev ballerina, Lydia Lopokova, as guest artist in the tiny role of the milkmaid, was first performed. It is today still in the repertoire of the Royal Ballet.

Two years earlier, a young man, working as an accountant with a firm in Smithfield Market, approached Marie Rambert and asked if he could take lessons. She admired his determination and his "poetic eyes" as she described them, later giving him the job of stage manager so that he could learn his craft. This was Antony Tudor who was during the following years to create his two masterpieces, *Dark Elegies* and *Lilac Garden*, for Ballet Rambert.

It is probably true to say that no choreographer of this century—not even Fokine himself—has had a more profound influence on the art of choreography. It is pervasive; one finds hints of his works, even the most distant echoes, in ballets of many different styles. It is, looking back, quite extraordinary that Marie Rambert should discover and encourage two young men who have, to a very large extent, been the most influential choreographers over some fifty years.

Ashton became a choreographer almost by accident; he wanted, above all, to be a great dancer. But Tudor had only one goal, and it is a tragedy for English Ballet that he was allowed to slip through our hands and build a great career in the United States. Had he been given a truly stable company to work with and dancers who understood his style and his method of composition, it is a matter of endless speculation how much more he might have achieved than a small handful of masterpieces. At the time of writing, the Royal Ballet performs none of his works, although they have been part of the repertoire of the American Ballet Theater for many years. It is a sad comment upon our national ballet that this should be so.

Even after forty years the beauty of *Lilac Garden* and *Dark Elegies* remains undimmed. Neither time nor changing fashion have taken anything from them; their compassion, intensity and the deep expressiveness of their images still haunt the mind with a kind of piercing beauty I know in no other modern works. *Lilac Garden* tells the story of a woman who tries to say farewell to her lover whom she has to abandon for a marriage of

17

convenience; at the same time her fiancé seeks to escape from the anguish of his abandoned mistress. Set in the twilight of a summer evening, the ballet aches with a sense of loss and ended love, where only sudden glances, whispers, the brief touch of hands are allowed before both couples are drawn back into the social world in which they live. If a kiss is given, it is snatched in a fleeting second; a smile exists only for the brief moment it is returned. There is a kind of desperation, the throbbing of hidden grief heard beneath the desolation of the music. In the ebb and flow of the dance all the sad secrecies of the heart are revealed in sudden insights that are unique in the history of modern ballet.

Dark Elegies, composed a year later in 1937, exposes the desolate grief of parents at the deaths of their children. It is set in a mood of elegiac lament, in movements of wide, sculptural beauty, ending on a note of quiet resignation; the dancers are heavy with their grief, burdened with a terrible anguish. In it there is a sense of the huge isolation of sorrow, the loneliness of the stricken heart. The dancers move in a kind of trance, inward regarding, alone. The ballet has a nobility and a compassion rarely seen in theatrical art; on the basis of these works alone, Antony Tudor takes up his rightful place as one of the few creators of genius in the history of the dance.

Shortly after composing this ballet, Tudor left the Company and formed his own group, later to become the London Ballet. However, by that time another superb choreographer had emerged. Andrée Howard had mounted her first ballet, *Our Lady's Juggler*, as early as 1933, and this was to be followed by a series of works, created with extraordinary delicacy and perception, as well as an acute sense of drama, among which were *Lady into Fox*, *Death and the Maiden* and *La Fête Etrange*, the latter first composed for Tudor's London Ballet. Acutely sensitive, Andrée Howard created works that seemed to shimmer in the light of the music, full of hints and delicate shading of emotions, subtle in colour and line, lit by an imagination that was sad and wondering, so that sometimes the ballets were seen as if through a glimmer of tears. A great ballet company, like Ballet Rambert, can never wholly escape its past, for it creates its own tradition, and it is fitting that Schubert's music from his string quartet, *Death and the Maiden*, should be used again by George Crumb in the sixth section of *Black Angels*.

With that uncanny ability for discovering and nurturing talent within her own ranks, Dame Marie Rambert encouraged one of her finest dancers, Frank Staff, towards choreography, as a result of which he composed two of the most delightful and durable works in the repertoire, *Peter and the Wolf* to Prokoviev's music and *Czernyana*, to the piano exercises of Czerny that have tormented generations of children. Each achieved enormous success, and *Peter and the Wolf* still lives on, its paint-box brilliance undimmed, in the repertoire of the Northern Dance Theatre.

It must have given Dame Marie great delight that one of her dancers in this extraordinarily rich period of the mid-thirties was Kyra Nijinsky, daughter of the immortal dancer whom Dame Marie had guided twenty years before through the intricacies of Stravinsky's music for *The Rite of Spring*. And it was right that her Company should be part of so living a tradition, since never in all her eagerness for experiment and the discovery of new talent has Dame Marie lost her devotion to the classical dance and to its greatest exponents. Ballet Rambert has always been the least insular of companies: the dancers have been encouraged to study the work of other groups, to learn from many different styles and approaches to the dance. It is this openness and intellectual daring that will never allow them to give a dull or routine performance, and this tradition continues today.

So many dancers in so many different companies show one only the classroom on stage; they dance, not to an audience, but to a wall of mirrors. The dancers of Ballet Rambert have always, even when they have been technically sometimes uncertain, given one the theatre. When performing the great classical roles, I have seen quite inexperienced young artists take the stage with all the aplomb and sense of theatrical magnetism of the greatest performers, and it was for this reason that I suspect the technical standards of the past were not as high as critics of those days imagined; they were, in fact, deceived by

19

all the duplicities of a theatrical art which the young dancers had learned—as they learn it today—from seeing themselves on the stage and not in the studio. Watching the dancers working on *Black Angels* in the bleak atmosphere of the classroom, it was astounding to observe how this tradition was maintained. One forgot the mirrors, the piano, the roar of traffic below; even in such a setting the dance was projected with the same intensity as it would later be seen in the theatre. So it was fifty years ago; so it is now.

With the war Ballet Rambert took on a new and exciting life. They amalgamated with Tudor's London Ballet and gave lunch and tea-time performances, mainly at the Arts Theatre in London, that became hugely popular. Sometimes they would give as many as five performances in one day; exhausted but happy, they brought a vivid splash of colour to the darkened city which neither bombs nor black-outs could dispel. New dancers were beginning to emerge, notably Sally Gilmour, who was to become the ballerina of the Company and its most notable artist for many years. Her wistful beauty, the poetry and delicacy of her dancing, the vividness of her imagination, are unforgettable. A superb actress with a huge dramatic range, she was also a dancer of exquisite musicality and line. Her dancing must still haunt many memories, as it does mine.

Under the sponsorship of C.E.M.A., a government body to encourage the arts, they travelled to army stations and factories, to reach a vast new public, most of whom had never seen ballet in their lives. They toured the country endlessly, dancing often on makeshift stages, in the bleak settings of munition factories and military camps. Apart from a sad interlude, brought about by legal difficulties over the rights in the Company when it was dancing at the Arts Theatre, that necessitated a suspension of work for some eighteen months, the war years created this new audience from which other companies were to benefit when peace came.

Ballet Rambert then began to give annual performances at Sadler's Wells Theatre which continue up to the present time; and though they were sometimes overshadowed by their grander and more opulent companion, the Sadler's Wells Ballet at

20

Covent Garden, they yielded to no one in style and the theatrical finish of their works. This was noticeable in their production of *Giselle*, first seen in its entirety in 1946 with Sally Gilmour in the title role. This has, in my experience, never been equalled in its exquisite evocation of the Romantic Age and the ballets of long ago. Since then we have seen fine productions, notably by the Bolshoi Ballet in 1956, the Festival Ballet and, most recently, the Scottish Ballet, but none for me combined warmth, humanity and understanding of the Romantic tradition as this version created thirty years ago.

For eighteen months from 1947 until 1949 the Company were engaged on a tour of Australia and New Zealand which, originally booked for six months, became continually extended due to their huge popularity. In many ways these were the most triumphant months in their history, but when they returned to London it was difficult to survive in competition with other richer companies that had now emerged. Then followed years of struggling against financial hardship, the loss of dancers to other groups, and, most serious of all, the departure of their then leading choreographer, Walter Gore, who had been one of the mainstays of the Company for twenty years.

The life-blood of Ballet Rambert has always been the presence of a true choreographer (of which there are very few) working regularly with the dancers, continually experimenting, in an atmosphere that offers artistic security. When Walter Gore left they were, in a sense, artistically stranded. This situation was not, of course, to continue indefinitely, since Dame Marie could discover talent from a random collection of people on the top of a bus, but the Company could not afford a period that was artistically sterile, even while it faced mounting financial difficulties. The dancers rallied round as ever; a new choreographer, Norman Morrice, emerged who was to have a profound influence on their future history, but this sense of insecurity undermined the confidence of the dancers. There is no virtue in poverty or financial embarrassment for a ballet company, but it has, over the years, produced its own compensations.

Ballet Rambert could, and does, survive on very little money;

21

it lives dangerously from one production to another, and if this puts the dancers under great pressure, it is also a spur to new endeavours and to the establishment of a corporate spirit which is one of its most remarkable features. Over the years its dancers have almost starved for it, and masterpieces have been created on empty stomachs. I do not believe in the romantic ideal of the starving artist, or even the hungry one, but at least it never leads to complacency and insularity to which other companies are sometimes prone.

Ballet Rambert could not afford to employ a sufficient number of dancers to perform all the large-scale works to which the public were by now attracted; at the same time the group had to be on tour for a considerable part of the year and employ the services of their own orchestra. The production of *Don Quixote* in 1962, in which the brilliant dancing of Lucette Aldous won great acclaim, was not sufficient to attract the large audiences that supported the Royal Ballet and Festival Ballet. Famous guest artists could not be engaged, and the lack of a permanent home, the smallness of their grants from the Arts Council, led to a position of near desperation in 1966.

For a considerable time before this they carried on as a result of promises of a new theatre being made available to them, even to the extent that plans were drawn up by Sir Basil Spence. Then the idea of a merger between Ballet Rambert and Festival Ballet foundered after protracted discussions. The continual travelling and the limitations of rehearsal hours made it impossible to mount the series of new works by which Ballet Rambert could, as in the past, attract and hold an audience.

After two years of doubt, of unfulfilled promises and shattered hopes, it was decided to reconstitute the Company on entirely new lines. This was to be a group of seventeen soloists, no *corps de ballet*, to concentrate on the creation of new works and the preservation of those from the past that would be suitable for them. Marie Rambert remained Director of this "new" Company, with Norman Morrice its associate director and chief choreographer. It was like starting from the beginning again, a concept much to Dame Marie's taste.

The first performance of this new company was given at the

Jeannetta Cochrane Theatre on 28th November, 1966. The "old" company had bowed out at the open air theatre in Holland Park on 2nd July, so that the intervening period was one of great activity as a new repertoire was learned and rehearsed. At the Jeannetta Cochrane the first night's ballets included two by Pierre Lacotte, *Numéros* and *Intermède*; *Time Base* by John Chesworth (another of Dame Marie's discoveries from among her dancers) and *Laiderette* by Kenneth Mac-Millan. The remainder of the repertoire was a skilful blending of the old and the new—*Judgement of Paris*, *Lilac Garden* and *Dark Elegies*, all by Antony Tudor; *Night Island* by the brilliant young Dutch choreographer, Rudi van Dantzig of the Nederlands Dans Theater—a company that had so much in common with the newly-formed Ballet Rambert—*Diversities* by Jonathan Taylor and *The Realms of Choice* by Norman Morrice.

During their opening tour Ballet Rambert had the double task of retaining their old audience and creating a new one which would be interested in modern, experimental works. There was some perplexity among those who had loved and followed the old Company with its repertoire that included such works as *Don Quixote*, *Coppélia* and *Giselle*; indeed some of them complained noisily that they had been betrayed. At the same time a new public grew up, mainly composed of young people who were on the whole scornful and dismissive of the great nineteenth-century classics that formed the basis of the repertoires of the big companies like the Royal Ballet and Festival Ballet.

Ballet Rambert remained a classically-based company, and the dancers studied classical and modern techniques, the latter formed mainly from the ideas of Martha Graham, at alternative classes, a procedure that is still followed today. In 1966 the teacher of classical dance was Eileen Ward and of modern dance Anna Price. Contrary to popular belief there is no real conflict between the two schools; indeed I have been told by Gary Sherwood, the present teacher of classical ballet with the Company, that they complement one another and strengthen the dancers technically.

This is an idea that has been slow in acceptance with the

23

larger companies; it is only very recently that the dancers of the Royal Ballet began to take classes in modern dance. On the other hand, those who are schooled only in the Graham-based technique have not the same capabilities as those from the classical school, so that it has become the practice of Ballet Rambert to engage dancers who have been classically trained. It is easier to extend the range of a classical dancer by teaching modern techniques than it is the other way round.

The wholly modern companies, such as the London Contemporary Dance Theatre have not, in my opinion, really proved their claims for an exclusively modern approach to the dance; indeed, although they have produced a large number of works, so that there may be as many as eight of these in one short season, they have not created ballets that have become standard additions to the repertoire as have Ballet Rambert with its more eclectic method of training. Indeed only one ballet created outside the classical tradition has survived for any length of time from the past, and that is Kurt Jooss' *The Green Table*; the remainder, while often fascinating when one first sees them, quickly fade away into oblivion.

In their first year under this new policy Ballet Rambert produced an astonishing figure of fourteen new ballets. Most significantly for the future, two of these, *Pierrot Lunaire* and *Ricercare*, were by the American choreographer, Glen Tetley, who has in recent years become perhaps the greatest single influence upon modern choreography. These two works remained in the repertoire, and were among the ballets given in the Company's anniversary season at Sadler's Wells in 1976. Five further ballets by Tetley have been added since, including *Ziggurat*, one of his greatest works which has rarely been out of the Company's programmes.

It seems to me, having watched Ballet Rambert's experimental seasons at the Jeannetta Cochrane Theatre, the first of which was in 1967, that every apprentice choreographer is almost obsessively influenced by Tetley. He had, of course, a profound influence on Christopher Bruce himself, though Bruce was to outgrow this and to find his own style which is highly individualistic, the expression of an intensely personal vision. At the

last experimental season, in 1976, ten new ballets were performed with choreography by dancers in the Company, and the
ideas of Tetley were pervasive in nearly all of them.

It is extraordinary, however, that from a Company of sixteen
dancers as there are at present, so many of these were able to
produce professional works, some of which were of a high
enough standard to form the basis of a new repertoire. It is true
that no original creative talent was to emerge, as Christopher
Bruce had emerged as a result of an earlier season, yet it gave
an indication of the seriousness and intellectual curiosity of the
Rambert dancers which make their dancing so creatively
exciting.

Glen Tetley has a wider range than any other living choreographer, so that he is able to move easily from works based
almost entirely on the Graham technique to those far more
classically orientated. At one extreme is *Ziggurat*, a ballet with
a kind of elemental force, in which primitive man emerges from
his baffling twilight, moving in an unfamiliar world, and
Voluntaries, composed for the Stuttgart Ballet, where the whole
creative process, the primal act of creation, is shown in
classically-designed choreography of amazing intensity. I consider *Voluntaries* to be one of the few masterpieces of twentieth-
century ballet, and I have written about it at length in my
previous book, *Images of the Dance*. In *Ziggurat*, Tetley has
been able to create dances in great blocks of movement, heavy
and stubborn as the earth over which the dancers so blindly
walk, groping towards the light of belief, creating their primitive
gods. In contrast, *Pierrot Lunaire* is a timeless ballet where
Clown and his Columbine symbolize all our yearnings and our
impossible dreams, as did the immortal figures of the Commedia
dell'Arte so many centuries ago.

Apart from Tetley and another American choreographer,
Anna Sokolow, who contributed two ballets, the impassioned
Deserts and *Opus 65*, the main creative work came from the
Company's own choreographers. In the two London seasons in
November, 1970, and May, 1971, four Rambert choreographers
contributed all five of the new works, two of which, Christopher
Bruce's *Wings* and Norman Morrice's *The Empty Suit*, were

mounted for companies overseas. In addition, John Chesworth had created his first ballets, including *H* and *Tic-Tack*, both premiered during Ballet Rambert's first west-end season at the Phoenix Theatre in 1968, and *Pawn to King 5*, composed the same year. John Chesworth was to play an increasingly important role in the Company's activities, and when Norman Morrice resigned as director in 1974 after twenty-one years with the Company, Chesworth succeeded him as Artistic Director. At the same time Christopher Bruce was appointed Associate Choreographer, to be made Associate Director the following year.

As well as seasons at the Sadler's Wells Theatre, Ballet Rambert broke new ground when they appeared on open stages and in the round, first at the Crucible Theatre, Sheffield, later at both the Young Vic and the Roundhouse. The close proximity of the audience with their different angles of vision added a new dimension to the choreography, and allowed the dancers to make fascinating adjustments to their performances in order that they should project in such intimate surroundings. The seasons have all been hugely successful, particularly among young people who found the intimacy in performance very close to their own ideas, which had been developed in theatres such as these and also in the tiny "fringe" theatres of London.

A further extension of Ballet Rambert's activities occurred in 1972 when the Rambert Dance Unit was formed under the direction of Ann Whitley to pioneer the Company's work in schools, colleges and those towns without a properly equipped theatre. Steadily a new audience was being formed, as devoted to Ballet Rambert as had been the audiences of earlier days. The Company filled an important gap between the large-scale organizations, such as the Royal Ballet and Festival Ballet with their emphasis on big classical works and the small, more esoteric dance groups whose style owed little to the classical tradition.

Apart from extended tours in the United Kingdom, the Company began to receive many invitations from abroad. They have danced at the Premio Roma Festival and the Israel Festival, both in 1970, at the Bergen Festival and the Kuopio

Dance Festival in Finland in 1971, as well as in many other countries. In 1975 they represented Britain at DANZA 75 in Venice, while the following year they took part in the Paris Festival of the Dance where *Black Angels* was seen for the first time abroad.

Always anxious to break new ground, since this had been a tradition of the Company since 1926, special performances were arranged for children which were hugely successful. *Bertram Batell's Sideshow* was greeted with shrill, indeed sometimes uproarious approval throughout the country, as was its successor, *Take a Running Jump*. The future, which has always been Dame Marie Rambert's only concern, was being secured. The Company is today, as she wishes it to be, a group of pioneers; its art is a perilous venture, never fully established, never truly secure. There are, after fifty years, sheafs of laurels to rest on, but the dancers are too busy, too involved even to glance back.

2. The Choreographer

Many choreographers have been good dancers, but it is rare indeed to find one who was more than that. One thinks at once of Léonide Massine, the wit, humanity and dazzling originality of whose dancing have made it so difficult for any other performer to follow him in his roles. He remains a solitary genius and he has left no successors, for genius makes its own laws, finds its own path up the mountainside. The leading choreographers of our time—Ashton, Tudor, Robbins and MacMillan—were never more than competent performers, but this did not matter to them for their aim was set in a different direction, the rare and difficult art they had chosen to follow. There are very few true choreographers, though there are large numbers who can set steps to music, just as in any age we find few poets though many versifiers, rhymers without number.

Christopher Bruce is a true choreographer; he is also a brilliant dancer, one of the finest in modern ballet. Indeed the very qualities one finds in his dancing—its intensity, musical comprehension and breadth of movement—are those that are most remarkable in his choreography. He manages somehow to follow these two parallel careers, and each, it seems to me, gains from the other; there is a constant interplay between the discoveries he makes as a dancer and those that go to enrich his choreography. I feel that, at this stage of his career, were he to give up dancing, as happens with most choreographers, his work would suffer as a result: both sides of his talent are creative and truly interrelate. Apart from Hans van Manen, I know of no young choreographer working in the contemporary theatre who is so gifted or has so wide a range or more searching an imagination.

Born in 1945, Christopher Bruce joined the Rambert School, and after graduating into the Company, quickly began to take on leading roles, one of which, that of the Clown in Glen Tetley's *Pierrot Lunaire* was to gain him wide recognition as one of the greatest dancers of our time. This was endorsed when he received the first *Evening Standard* award for Ballet.

He was fortunate in that his rise to principal dancer coincided with the decision, taken in 1966, for the Company to make a radical break from its famous past. There were many (including

31

myself) who mourned the loss of so great a repertoire that contained ballets by Tudor, Andrée Howard, Ashton, Frank Staff and Ninette de Valois, which it seemed still had artistic relevance as well as being works of real distinction and historical importance. However, the demand for new ballets made the directors of the Company search out new talent. Apart from mounting works from outside choreographers, they sought for these within their own ranks, so that experimental seasons of workshop performances of ballets by apprentice choreographers were instigated and indeed continue to the present day. One of the choreographers to emerge was Christopher Bruce.

His first work, *George Frideric*, composed in 1969 to Handel's D major violin sonata, was in fact something of a surprise. Classically designed mainly on the academic technique, it was cool, professional, even understated. The ballet was highly musical, intricately balanced, but only in the free use of the arms and upper torso did it indicate a truly individual insight into movement. The quality of the dance was relaxed, with long *legato* phrasing of each *enchaînement*; indeed one sensed the influence of the new plasticity in style, developed by Agrippina Vaganova, that we had witnessed in the dancing of Galina Ulanova and members of the Bolshoi Ballet in their first, historic season at Covent Garden.

Composed for six dancers, *George Frideric* is a kind of chamber music for ballet, recalling in its even flow and moments of sudden poetry music written for small groups of wind instruments by Mozart and Schubert. At the conclusion of the ballet the dancers flounce off with the same kind of abrupt finality that these composers use to end their chamber works. One had expected something more daring, more naïve; this kind of cool assurance seemed more to belong to an established choreographer relaxing in a minor work.

Christopher Bruce's second ballet, a *pas de deux* for himself and Sandra Craig, *Living Space*, created later in the same year, is a work of great originality, vehemence and controlled passion; indeed it reminded me at times of Roland Petit's *Le Jeune Homme et la Mort*, composed for Jean Babilée. Instead of music Bruce uses the music of words—a prose poem by

Robert Cockburn, marvellously orchestrated by the choreographer as a pattern for dancing. Sometimes the dance follows the rhythm of the words, at others it relates in counterpoint; throughout the work we are conscious of the shifting relationship between the couple, varying from tenderness to anger and hostility and moments of beautiful reconciliation. In a way it anticipates Hans van Manen's superb *pas de deux*, *Twilight*, in its study of the bitterness and sad alienation between two young people in love, a theme also explored by Jerome Robbins in his exquisite series of *pas de deux*, *In the Night*. The influence of Tetley was clearly apparent, yet *Living Space* was a highly personal vision which threw long shadows into the future. In this ballet Christopher Bruce found his own voice.

Bruce's third work, *Wings*, was composed not for the Ballet Rambert but for the Ballet Company of the Bühnen der Stadt, Cologne in 1970. It was not taken into the Rambert repertoire until the following year, since which time it has won an enduring place in its programmes, and is perhaps the most admired of all his ballets. Certainly it marked the emergence of a major talent, with a vision of life that was in certain ways cold and uncompromising, that looked for no easy solution to the loneliness of human encounters, nor tried to soften the sense of alienation that is so much a feature of his art.

The initial inspiration was contained in certain images of flight in Glen Tetley's ballet, *Ziggurat*, which Bruce sought to develop into a full-length work. It appears to be set in an empty world, when there is no consciousness, only an instinctive groping for light as the long progress of evolution begins. There is no sun, no moon; only the icy twilight of an unawakened world where these strange winged creatures hover over the dark edge of time.

The ballet can be seen on two levels: in images of flight, predatory and instinctive; but also as a study of the conflict and sad isolation of men and women in their secret lives. The men are panic stricken; they beat at the air, swoop aimlessly towards the void, fall defeated to the ground. The girls are cold and loveless; if they suffer, they hold their grief within, and seem to lack the terrible vulnerability of the men. Between the two groups in the ballet there is no meeting; each remains alone, sometimes, it seems, hardly aware of the other; indeed the first greeting, the first touch between the dancers that has some trace of human warmth is between two men, here clinging to one another in terrible isolation.

The electronic score, commissioned by Christopher Bruce from Bob Downes, echoes coldly like the wind blowing round the dead stars. In many ways *Wings* is a disturbing ballet, for nowhere does it offer any comfort; it has the terrible sense that even now we may be groping towards one another in such an icy twilight, where there is only the darkness and no dawn. It is an extraordinary work, loveless as the cold moon.

From the primitive anguish of *Wings*, in his next two works Bruce turned to the particular horrors of war. His personal revulsion against the bestialities of war is, of course, common to all sensitive people, but in his case it was intensified by the fact that his father had been seriously wounded, so that for many years he lived in pain and disability. *For these who die as cattle*, composed in 1972, runs parallel to a famous poem by Wilfred Owen, that great poet who himself perished in the first world war:

> What passing-bells for these who die as cattle?
> Only the monstrous anger of the guns.
> Only the stuttering rifles' rapid rattle
> Can patter out their hasty orisons.
> No mockeries now for them; no prayers nor bells,
> Nor any voice of mourning save the choirs,—
> The shrill, demented choirs of wailing shells;
> And bugles calling for them from sad shires.
>
> What candles may be held to speed them all?
> Not in the hands of boys, but in their eyes
> Shall shine the holy glimmers of good-byes.
> The pallor of girls' brows shall be their pall;
> The flowers the tenderness of patient minds,
> And each slow dusk a drawing-down of blinds.

There have been many ballets about the horrors and stupidities of war, the most famous being Kurt Jooss' *The Green*

Table which incorporates the antics of politicians and statesmen who cavort so grotesquely away from the dead, and are so bitterly assailed by Siegfried Sassoon, who was Owen's friend and mentor, in his poetry. *The Green Table* takes place round the baize-topped table where the statesmen meet, prancing and gesticulating, while Death stalks through the fields of battle beyond their vision. A later work on the theme of the bestiality of war is Antony Tudor's *Echoing of Trumpets*, a masterly piece revived for the Festival Ballet, yet too explicit in imagery, indeed in a certain obviousness of style that is quite untypical of the most subtle of all choreographers, for it to make more than a shock impact.

In his ballet Bruce shows us the encounter between four soldiers and Death, together with the two women who mourn for them, eternal figures who have mourned all our centuries away. There is no music; only the stamping of feet in the ritual dance of war. The figure of Death moves around them, watches with cold indifference, even, it seems, sometimes with contempt. The dances are stark and angular, set to primitive images, the men crouched in *demi-plié* (an increasingly frequent image in Bruce's work) like the design of some ancient cave painting.

His second work on this theme, *There Was a Time*, first performed at the Young Vic in 1973, was an attempt to encapsulate the ancient Greek narrative concerning the Trojan War as seen with the eyes of Zeus from Olympus. Here the choreographer seeks to universalize his theme where the figures of Hector, Achilles and Paris exist on a symbolic level, the sport and playthings of the gods. Some critics complained that the work was confused and difficult to follow, though the Pyrrhic dances of battle had great power, while the groupings had something of the chaste beauty of a Grecian frieze.

After a series of works of such stark emotion, in his next ballet, *Duets*, composed in the latter part of 1973, Bruce reverted to the more classical and decorative style of *George Frideric*. Here we watch a series of encounters between three couples that are far lighter in mood, having indeed something in common with Jerome Robbins' *Dances at a Gathering* and van Manen's marvellous *Four Schumann Pieces*, later performed

35

by the Royal Ballet. The work is structured on a technical device whereby each dancer takes up the same movement as his or her predecessor, to achieve a kind of fugal effect. To my mind this becomes increasingly monotonous, once one has grasped the style, and in many ways I consider this to be the least successful of his works, though the composition of the individual dances has great structural beauty and a sense of line almost sculptural in its proportions.

Two ballets followed in 1974, *Unfamiliar Playground,* Christopher Bruce's first work to be created for the Royal Ballet, and *Weekend,* first performed at the Roundhouse in April of that year. In *Unfamiliar Playground,* danced by a Company trained in the pure academic technique, Bruce achieved a brilliant synthesis between this and the free style of the Rambert dancers. Emotionally the ballet marked a return to the intensity of expression and mature insight into human relations of *Wings,* while the structure handled group and solo dances with masterly precision.

Composed for five men and five girls, in this ballet there is no sense of interplay between the sexes. In the first two episodes of the ballet the men dance alone, then to be followed by the girls. Any approach between them is made with no sign of tenderness; instead, each dancer is isolated in a kind of rapt self-absorption that is icily exclusive. Emotionally it is a bleak work, but as a study of the tension that exists between men and women in so many of their encounters, it is a mature judgement of frightening objectivity. It is as if the dances were set in some bleak landscape where there only exists the cold solitude of unloved hearts. *Unfamiliar Playground* is a ballet that is entirely contemporary in spirit, a parable of our own harsh and mechanistic age. It is like a game played by abandoned children in the last light of the world.

In a sense *Unfamiliar Playground* is complementary to *Wings* to the extent that, while *Wings* looks at the most distant past, *Unfamiliar Playground* reaches towards an equally remote future. It is a world lit by a cold lunar light, devoid of human warmth, set in that empty hour before all falls into chaos, a vacancy illuminated only by the last stars. The futuristic concept of the *décor* by Nadine Baylis expresses the same idea, where the silver body-tights worn by the dancers are reminiscent of cosmonauts' suits, and the bare scaffolding hints at a wholly functional universe. In the writhing of limbs and arms is the image of primitive life that slowly begins to engulf these last survivors of the cold earth, who will then sink into darkness, and the great evolutionary cycle, symbolized in *Wings*, will begin again. For that reason the stage is empty when the curtain falls—vacant, like the unpeopled earth.

The expressive range of Bruce's choreography reached a new level of intensity in *Weekend*, in my view perhaps the finest of all his works to date. Here the interchange between five dancers is sustained on a level of barely-controlled passion, ranging from eroticism to hostility and rejection, in a manner that is accentuated by the unequal distribution of roles between two men and three girls. Throughout the ballet the electronic music of Brian Hodgson throbs with the endless beating of the heart, around which is heard the sound of the wind, the hiss of the driving rain.

The five of them meet in a series of brutal encounters where tenderness is shown only in a kind of sad compassion for one another, a sudden greeting in their eyes, as if their loneliness were the one experience they truly shared. One is reminded of Rilke's beautiful statement in his letters: "Love is when two solitudes touch and greet one another." Because of the unequal balance of the roles a single girl is often left as an outsider, and I recall a remark by that fine novelist, Doris Lessing, who said that she hears from women now one note only, continually repeated, the voice of themselves betrayed.

Few ballets in my experience open so dramatically. In a long shaft of light from the wings a man and a girl enter from opposite sides of the stage. Slowly they approach one another, meeting at last in a kind of despairing embrace. In the unfolding of each separate pose, very even and deliberate, as if filmed in slow motion, one sees the awakening of a love in which they hardly dare to believe. They dance a series of steps, very fast, then as suddenly broken off, which are like stabs of feeling, spasms of the heart, which die almost before they are known.

38

This change from slow motion to fast, jagged movement has an extraordinary effect of sudden violence, like a discord in music.

In poses the dancers are enfolded around one another in two curves, like a pair of broken arches; now and again the hands intertwine to give a sudden delicacy to each image, as if on a statue a scatter of blossoms fell. Continually the eye is arrested by exquisitely proportioned designs, where the space between the dancers is exactly calculated to hold their poses, each in balance with the other. At one moment, for example, two girls sit backstage left, each with one knee raised and their hands upon it, while the male dancer, equidistant and front stage right, dances before their cold appraising stare. Put as geometrically as this, one can gain no idea of the beauty of such proportions, the sense of measure and total design. In another disturbing section two girls dance a *pas de deux*, yet one senses that they are rivals, even enemies, drawn together with a cold reluctance.

It is a feature of Bruce's choreography that he will give emphasis to certain images, so that they almost become *leitmotifs* in the dancing. This is clearly the case in *Weekend* where the men will fling their arms at a steep angle above them, while the body is held upright in a kind of preening gesture; the girls' movements often turn inwards, the body crouched, the arms held forwards and curved like wings. This seems to me to make a fine distinction between the extrovert almost flamboyant (and certainly aggressive) character of the men and the introverted attitude of the girls that is both passive and wary. One might describe it as a further development of Fokine's distinction between movements performed *en dedans* and *en dehors*, each indicating contrasted emotional attitudes. It is also a contrast between two traditions that meet in Christopher Bruce's ballets, those of the open classical dance and those of the modern dance which is centred inwardly on the body.

Weekend is concerned with physical passion and eroticism, also the desperate need to love, to awaken the estranged heart. One has the feeling of a separation and a coming together again, when periods of absence are followed by a return to the person loved, now distant in her new-found solitude. Here a mutual adjustment has to be made, where the independence, even the loneliness of absence, has to be transcended in a common love. At first this is difficult; sometimes there may even be cruelty in it, a kind of resentment, and the sad irony is that when this union has been achieved, it has to be broken again. This, of course, is a common experience among dancers and theatrical performers who, when they are on tour, have only the weekend to re-establish their relationships with those they love. It is with such emotions that Christopher Bruce here deals in choreography of complex brilliance and poignant intensity.

One remembers, towards the end of the ballet, how one passage of dancing is dazzlingly orchestrated so that each performer dances a different series of steps, but all relate to the total pattern. The rather obvious fugal technique of *Duets* which I mentioned earlier has been replaced by the most subtle counterpoint in movement, one quite astonishing in its daring. After this passage the girls leave the men. They shiver with cold, try to warm themselves, hugging their bodies with their arms. The weekend is over. When the five dancers part, the girls drop a sad distortion of a curtsey that bleakly echoes the farewell of the dancers in Robbins' *Dances at a Gathering*. The man and the girl are now left alone; sadly they part also, leaving the empty stage abandoned to the sound of rain and the conniving wind.

I have dealt with this work in far greater detail than I intended, but it contains such richness of movement, so wide a range of emotion that it cannot be easily dismissed in a few words. It is a piece of fine theatre, but it is more than that; it is, as I suppose all art should be, a criticism of life and our own times. We live, many of us, in what could be described as weekend relationships: it is the truth of these that Christopher Bruce seeks to explore.

The last ballet he has composed, *Ancient Voices of Children*, to music of that title by George Crumb, was first performed at Sadler's Wells in July, 1975. It is the most poetic of all his works to date, matching throughout the poems of Lorca which were the composer's inspiration. The ballet appears to be set on some sun-bleached plain, wide and featureless, that is so much a part of the Spanish landscape. It has a great sense of space, contained also in the music, where each gesture the dancers make seems dwarfed by such great horizons, the impersonality of the empty world around them.

We see the people waking, loving, grieving, bearing children and dying; then all who remain return to sleep, so that the whole ballet is contained within the image of a single day. It holds stark and beautiful images—one in particular, when a girl is carried, like a broken doll, in diagonal across the stage, the line of her body continued by the cape trailing from her hand; a second girl joins this sad procession, following it slowly out of sight.

Here in a grotesque funeral procession is the world of Goya, where the sly mourners mock at grief like the comforters in de Valois' *Job*; a child dances a game of hopscotch; a male dancer for a moment sketches a *veronica* on the air. All is drawn against the wide background of the music, the landscape it prefigures. *Ancient Voices of Children* contains nothing but essential images—a sketch in a few lines that invokes a country, a people and the tragedy and splendour of their history.

There were complaints that it did not have enough dancing, but, in fact, it is all dancing; as a raised arm is dancing, the turn of the head, a small movement with one leg, if they are placed exactly by the choreographer as a detail in a whole design. If complexity of movement, a gathering intensity of emotion were right for *Weekend*, so here the simplicity of the gestures, the fragments of broken dance, a few images of grief were right for *Ancient Voices of Children*. The music demanded it; it calls for space around the dancers, where each image must be set in a wide silence, the deserted land. It is, to my mind, a great work; a people and a history—their life in one day.

This must, of necessity, be a brief glance at Christopher Bruce's ballets, for I wanted to set his new work, not in isolation, but as another stage in his development as a choreographer. It has, remarkably, covered a span of less than eight years, while it shows a range of themes and styles that might be expected from a choreographer of much longer experience. His ballets are serious and deeply considered with a style that is very much his

41

own, so that each new work is a discovery, an adventure into an unknown land.

Christopher Bruce has thought deeply about the nature of his art, and in discussing this with him one becomes aware of a mind not caged in by theory, at once both pragmatic and searching.

"There are no hard and fast rules about choreography. The freedom an artist must have is limitless."

When Christopher Bruce said that to me, I realized how this quest for imaginative freedom is central to the ideas of so many artists—dancers, musicians, writers and painters—with whom I have spoken, and how far distant it is from the world of the critic who seeks to categorize and define. For this reason an artist finds it difficult to speak about his work, since immediately he does so in a way he diminishes it, places around it barriers of theory and technique that cannot enclose the truths of his art. "I always shy away from people who try and restrict you by theory," Bruce says. "Unless you are prepared to accept the limitlessness of what you can actually do as an artist, you will never achieve real creative work."

I did not come to him to discuss theories about his art or that of other choreographers, so much as try to glimpse (for one can do no more than that) the first spark of the creative process. And here again, it seems to me, all artists have much in common: in the beginning it is not the word but the image; from this the whole work expands and flowers. Dame Ninette de Valois puts this very finely when she says, "There must be an image; it is the spirit behind all choreography; and once projected it is developed, or replaced by another that shows some form of progress in time."

Christopher Bruce expressed the same idea when he said to me, "I start with a feeling about the quality of the movement, a single image. This is used as a basis for development, even though this first image may be later abandoned as no longer relating to that particular section of the dance. When I have completed one movement, I know intuitively the movement that should come next." He emphasizes that this is an instinctive sense, a feeling that the completed image is right and could not

42

be expressed in any other way. "It grows; it grows like life, organically." An artist becomes impatient if you try to define this sense of the rightness of what he has created, for it is felt on a level far deeper than reason.

It is, I think, the suddenness of the creative act that brings the greatest joy to the artist; the image springs into his mind like a new discovery, a moment's insight for which he is not prepared. It is for this that Christopher Bruce is continually searching. "Creation is discovery. I hate repeating myself, but always seek to discover new things, new ways of seeing, things even that take me by surprise. Each ballet must have a constant style and feeling of its own, and is somehow different, and hopefully very different, from all the others one has made." In the same way he wishes to surprise the dancers with whom he works: "I don't want to be predictable, either to the dancers or myself, so that I like to surprise them, in this way to keep their imaginations fresh and alive and give them a constant creative interest in the work."

It is not so much that he aims to express any particular emotion by the steps of the dance he creates, but rather to draw from the unconscious, the very depths of the personality, those images that have a meaning for himself. "If it does not come instinctively and from deep in the unconscious, it is probably not right. You can only delve. What comes out, comes out. You must use your choreographic technique to control this instinctive expression of deep emotion, give it form and set it within the work." Continually Christopher Bruce reverts to this idea, this sense of the free flowing of imagery from the depths of the personality, in a manner that is the natural expression of the inner life. I am reminded of Keats's magnificent remark in one of his letters: "If poetry comes not as naturally as the leaves to a tree, it had better not come at all."

This continual quest for freshness of vision, one that will come as a surprise not only to the dancers but also to himself, demands that Bruce should not, as it were, over-prepare his imagination. "Before I started the choreography and was just listening to the music, I would make notes, consider various ideas and images that arose from the music, but I knew from

43

experience it would happen differently. Often in the studio I would try out these ideas, but they always looked like *clichés*; they had no real life in them. If a thing has been in your head a long time it does not look fresh to you; it appears contrived. What you invent must be out of nothing, out of that time, that moment; it must be new, astonishing even to yourself, otherwise you've come up with something hackneyed and unoriginal. And one must be original every time you do something."

The images, considered in isolation, away from the studio and the dancers, lack so often the spontaneity of true creation. "If I write them down, try to describe them to myself, they become formalized and set. I must feel free and uncluttered in my imagination when I begin to create, with no preconceptions at all." This attitude is in many ways similar to the one expressed to me by Nadine Baylis when she described choreography as a personal encounter between the choreographer, the dancers and the music—a kind of perilous adventure, an exploration into a new land.

Often when he tried to sleep at night, Bruce told me, his mind would become filled with images of dancers, new groupings, new poses. "I felt the images, rather than saw them." He described to me how "they come when your mind is very free, just floating; sometimes I'd write them down. I could not sleep for hours until I determined not to be bothered by them any more." Yet in the morning they would often seem to him to be meaningless, now set down coldly, no longer a part of the creative process.

It is for this reason that Bruce chooses not to have preconceptions, ideas already worked out, but to grasp the intuitions of each moment, achieved by the free interplay between himself, the music and the dancers. It is, of course, one of the great problems of choreography that the actual material of the art is the human body, human beings with their different temperaments and different views of life. Yet it is from these conflicts, these reconciliations between his vision and their way of apprehending it, that the images are formed.

Bruce does not describe the quality of the movement to the dancers, or talk much about the emotions conveyed in any particular section of the ballet, or, indeed, its underlying ideas. This is something they must find out for themselves and create in their own way. On the other hand he does not seek their ideas for his own use, rather in the manner that certain choreographers, of whom Ashton is the prime example, will ask the dancers to improvise or suggest movements; it is more the personal way in which they express his concepts that may give him a new set of images. "Sometimes they will go into the next movement, and they are feeling it as I am feeling it too, and from this a new image may be formed. Sometimes a dancer does not do what you wanted him to do, not exactly; he takes your imagination up another path, and you like that path, so that the ballet subtly changes course." Indeed it is in these moments of spontaneous creation that the true artistic delight is found. "This" (he says) "is marvellous: the ballet is not how you imagined it at first. It is going to be something new, original, something which you could never have envisaged, different from anything you had ever seen or anyone else had ever seen."

In the studio Bruce will first try out an image and variations upon it by performing it himself; then he will form it on the dancers, so that in the coming together of these two different angles the design is formed, a constant interplay between the inner and the outer vision of the movement. It is, he says, a great advantage to work with dancers one knows, whose quality of movement one understands; but "one should not know them too well". There must always be aspects of their personalities that emerge in the dance that will be a discovery to him, as indeed to themselves; and it is this communication between his inner world and their personal expression of it that is the divine spark of choreography.

Christopher Bruce is only too well aware of the limitations of the medium in which he works, but this, he believes, is true of all artists; neither the word nor the dance is fully able to express the image. At best there can only be approximations, hints at a truth that is fundamentally incommunicable. "If I could find the words, I don't think I would be a choreographer, I'd be a novelist"; yet, even while he considers this, Bruce has to admit wryly that words are as inadequate as the human body to express the artist's vision. The choreographer, like the poets, knows that what he seeks to grasp is always just beyond his reach; as Eliot puts it:

> . . . and every attempt
> is a wholly new start, and a different kind of failure.

When working on the ballet, it is crucially important for Bruce to feel that he is stimulating the imagination of his dancers, that they are excited by what they do; it is their creativity as much as his own with which he is concerned, and when he feels he has reached this it aids him creatively. "That gives me confidence, makes me believe. And if I don't obtain this from the dancers, I am inclined to lose heart."

The confidence of an artist is a fragile thing; maybe, indeed, more so in the case of a choreographer who works exposed to others. If he is going to despair at his work, he is not like the writer or painter who can throw it on the fire; he cannot, much as sometimes he might like to do so, jettison his dancers out of the studio window. All the time he is observed even as he creates, and this is hard for him. Like all artists he loses confidence in his gifts, fears that he will dry up, have nothing more to say. Although Bruce does not seek advice either from his dancers or his colleagues about the work as he creates it, knowing that he must solve his problems alone, at the same time there are a few people, such as Nadine Baylis, his designer, whose comments upon his work are valuable to him and whose judgement he respects. "I need confidence like any artist: I am all too aware how fragile the border line is between success and failure, how easy it is to lose one's grip, and, once lost, it is difficult to regain."

When I asked Christopher Bruce what was the source of his inspiration, he indicated with his arm the street outside, people walking in the dazzling light of the early afternoon. "A man walks down the street," he said. "One notes the way he carries his head, the gestures he makes, his own personal mannerisms. All these are balletic, dance in its basic form. Dance, however abstract, is an expression of feelings, a way of looking at the

46

world." And this, I think, is the most remarkable feature of his choreography—its compassion and humanity, its concern for what is real in human relations, no mere abstraction, a question of cold form or lines drawn on the indifferent air.

He is not always in sympathy with some choreographers who equate the dance with mere abstract patterning; for him it is an expression of his own nature, his experience of life and the lives of others—the basis of his inspiration for the remarkable ballet *Weekend*—distilled into a compression of imagery whose source is hidden from himself. "I collect images," he said. "I store them up." These are images drawn from life and his own personal relationships, and also those from the ballets of other choreographers which he assimilates, to be absorbed into his own unconscious life, where he may find them, perhaps years later, transmuted and ready to take their place in a new ballet. "You dream, and your dreams are full of the memories of other ballets."

Bruce agrees that he has been very fortunate to develop as an artist in a Company that has invited so many choreographers from outside to create ballets for it, particularly since the Company was reformed as a modern dance group in 1966. "I sometimes lack faith in myself," he says. "I realize I can learn from other choreographers. You must not shut yourself off from outside influences, either in ballet or life, enclose yourself in your own world as sometimes artists do, and thus begin to limit yourself. You don't grow; you don't develop, and without this you might become sterile as an artist." His studies of the Graham technique have been of profound value to him, and he deeply admires the expressiveness and beautiful clarity of Martha Graham's choreography.

The most profound influence upon him has been the work of Glen Tetley, whose ballets he admires and respects, as he does Tetley's integrity as an artist. His early ballets were much under the influence of this great choreographer, with whom he worked on many occasions as a dancer in the closest harmony. He has now developed his own personal style, but he readily acknowledges how profoundly Tetley influenced his early work. Other choreographers with whom he has worked and for whom he has

great respect include Louis Falco and Anna Sokolow. From Falco, Christopher Bruce was able to gain a closer understanding of the modern dance idiom of José Limón which has had a far-ranging influence in the United States, although it is very little known in this country.

Like all choreographers working in the classical tradition (however much it has assimilated the ideas of the modern dance) Bruce recognizes Michel Fokine as a powerful influence, feeling no basic contradiction between his ballets and those of Merce Cunningham which have also affected him as a choreographer. Christopher Bruce is the least doctrinaire of choreographers, an attitude not always shared by his fellow artists, both of the past and our own time. He has great respect for classicism, and for those choreographers like Jerome Robbins who work mainly in classical forms; indeed it is one of his ambitions to create a ballet that would be totally classical, just as he also wishes to compose one that grew almost entirely from the modern school of the dance. He realizes that it is not likely he would be able to reach the extreme limits of either form, and that his work will remain a compromise between the two schools, leaning more heavily towards one or the other.

His *Unfamiliar Playground*, created for the classically-trained dancers of the Royal Ballet, shows his respect for the old tradition of the dance, and one senses in him none of the iconoclasm of some choreographers of the modern school who preach against classicism with a kind of religious fervour, this being particularly noticeable in those of earlier generations and, fortunately, not so prevalent in modern companies where there is a free exchange of ideas. One of the choreographers for the London Contemporary Dance Company, Robert North, has, for example, created two works for Ballet Rambert, and the Rambert dancers have great respect for him. Modern ballet now lives in a kind of artistic ecumenical age, and heresy hunts are something of the past.

Christopher Bruce believes that the standard of choreography is, on the whole, higher today than it was when he composed his first ballet, *George Frideric*, in 1969. As a result of the various workshop productions of Ballet Rambert, he thinks

49

that a number of promising choreographers might very well be developed from within the Company, although he accepts that choreography makes great demands in concentration and technique, so that beginners have often not the stamina to continue their careers. "One has to develop a certain skill, learn a language and an ability to construct well, otherwise you won't be a choreographer, however powerful your imagination or sensitivity. You must use your choreographic technique to control and shape your imagination, and this is hard and makes many demands, both intellectual and physical."

He does not feel that it is essential for the audience to understand completely what the choreographer wishes to convey. There should be a certain ambiguity, a level of different meanings in a work, and the audience will understand it in their own way. Indeed they may well find in it something new which the choreographer had not realized himself while creating the ballet. In this, of course, Bruce is at one with the poet who believes that the compression of imagery and many levels of meaning are central to his art. I am reminded of T. S. Eliot who, when asked about the meaning of one of his poems, would send the inquirer to Helen Gardner who, he maintained, understood his work better than he did himself.

The basis of choreography is difficult to understand since it rises from the artist's unconscious life, giving him material which, until that moment, he did not realize he owned. This element of surprise in creation, to which Bruce often refers, indicates the creative vitality of the artist, who is not concerned with his work on a superficial level, merely as a theatrical artifice, but as an expression of his deepest feelings and desires. Ultimately he must work for himself alone, recalling Stravinsky's remark when asked for whom he wrote his music: "I write it for myself" (he said) "and for one hypothetical other."

Maybe, looking back on our conversation, I have not penetrated far into the source of an artist's inspiration, but it is right that it should remain a mystery. It will, I suspect, always be so, both to the public and the artist himself, for he deals in strange harmonies and things that are beyond our understanding. It is wise to accept this, and to live content with mysteries.

50

3. The Music

Much contemporary music has been indicted, not without some reason, on two separate counts: first, that it is sterile and academic, of interest mainly to the musicologist; and secondly, that it is often ugly and cacophonous, speaking a private language inaccessible to the listener. It is, of course, not surprising that a century so brutal and mechanistic in many aspects of its life as our own should find this reflected in its art, not only in music but also in painting and literature. The despair of language as a form of communication is clearly evident in novels like *Finnegans Wake* and the plays of Samuel Beckett, in the same way as the years of war and tyranny shadow some of the works of Picasso, of all artists perhaps the truest chronicler of his age.

It is a sad irony that the century of mass communication—by radio, television and the press—is the one in which artists have most deeply retreated, out of despair or disgust, into the world of their secret imagination, even to the extent of believing that communication between the artist and his public is no longer possible. In the drama the Theatre of the Absurd and the Theatre of Cruelty exist as two manifestations of this despair, and one must see certain aspects of the contemporary dance in the same light, so far removed are they from the warmth and compassion, the wide humanity of works by older choreographers such as Massine and Tudor, not so much as being unintelligible as in not caring to be understood.

It is against this background that the music of George Crumb and the choreography of Christopher Bruce, who has found in it the source of his finest inspiration, must be judged. They have both within them many tragic insights, but they communicate on a deep, human level that is far removed from the academic or the language of private meditation. As the initial inspiration for the ballet, *Black Angels*, was found by the choreographer in the music, it is appropriate that this should be considered first.

George Crumb, who was born in West Virginia in 1929, is now Professor of Music at the University of Pennsylvania. He has been much honoured in his own country, having been awarded a Guggenheim Fellowship, the Composition Prize of the Broadcast Music Inc., the Koussevitzky International

Recording Award, the International Rostrum of Composers Award (UNESCO) and the Pulitzer Prize for Music in 1968. His principal works are as follows:

String Quartet, 1954; *Sonata for Solo Violincello*, 1955; *Variazioni* (for large orch.), 1959; *Five Pieces* (for piano), 1962; *Night Music I* (for soprano, keyboard and percussion), 1963; *Four Nocturnes Night Music II* (for violin and piano), 1964; *Madrigals, Books I and II*, 1965 (for solo voice and instruments); *Eleven Echoes of Autumn*, 1965 (for violin, alto flute, clarinet and piano), 1966; *Echoes of Time and the River* (Pulitzer prize 1968), 1967; *Songs, Drones and Refrains of Death* for baritone and electric instruments, 1968; *Madrigals, Books III and IV* for soprano and instruments, 1969; *Night of the Four Moons* for alto and instruments, 1969; *Black Angels (Thirteen Images from the Dark Land)* for electric string quartet, 1970; *Ancient Voices of Children* for soprano and instruments, 1970; *Vox Balaenae* for electric flute, electric cello and electric piano, 1971; *Lux Aeterna* for soprano, sitar, bass flute and two percussionists, 1971; *Makrokosmos Vol. I*, 1972, *Vol. II*, 1973.

To those willing to enter into it, the music of George Crumb, strange though it may seem at first, is in no manner remote or impersonal. It is often eerily lit, fearful and solitary, singing in mysterious harmonies, and yet it exists on a level of intense emotional expression, haunting and often tragic, with a compassionate insight that is rare indeed in contemporary art. This is the music of one who has looked deep into his own heart and into our own.

In the directions he has written on his scores Crumb has made no secret of his aim to communicate in this way. On one score he directs the pianist to play "eerily, with a sense of malignant evil"; or else, "musingly, like the gentle caress of a faintly remembered music". Elsewhere he asks that a score should be played "tenderly, hauntingly, as if from afar"; or, "incredibly soft, almost inaudible (with) sparse, wispy textures"; or "languidly, with a sense of loneliness". This sets him apart from most of his contemporaries whose music is more coldly conceived, and who would be unlikely to ask it to be expressed in such emotional terms.

George Crumb is essentially a dramatist, whose work is often closer to the tone poem than to the intellectualism of those composers whose use of serialism has, in my view, led to the aridity of a great deal of modern music. If one were to seek in his music for possible influences, these would be in the broad stream of romanticism. He recognizes his debt to Bartók, Mahler and Debussy; indeed in the latter's fastidious quest for new discoveries in tonality, he is probably the closest of all modern composers to the spirit in which Crumb's music is created. It is also interesting that the vocal technique of *sprechstimme* (a combination of song and speech) used by Schoenberg in *Pierrot Lunaire* has been incorporated into sections of Crumb's music, while *Pierrot Lunaire* has been choreographed by Glen Tetley for Ballet Rambert, the leading role being danced to dazzling effect by Christopher Bruce. It is a link between two composers and two choreographers whose work, in its sense of distance, loneliness and cold spaces, seems to have grown from a common source.

What above all Crumb appears to seek in his music is emotional intensity, a compression of images that bind his work together. In Alban Berg's splendid phrase, it is music composed from "ecstasies of logic". One will not find much melody or an elaborate use of counterpoint in Crumb's music, still less the formal development of ideas that is expected from composers of an earlier generation; instead there is this constant search for new realms in tonality, a feeling that the composer mixes his tones in the same manner as a painter mixes his palette. In a sense it is surrealist music, where the images clash violently together in a relation of opposites, to create this strange dream landscape he inhabits. It is a concern to let the images, whether of the poem or music, follow their own direction, even at the expense of formal design.

The first loyalty of such an artist is to the image itself, which must be nursed out of its own darkness, not by the clear light of reason but in the flickering shadows of intuition; it must be felt and lived, rather than invented. The composer puts this explicitly when he writes, "While composing *Makrokosmos*, I was aware of certain recurrent haunting images. At times quite vivid, at times vague and almost subliminal, these images seemed to coalesce around . . . several ideas (given in no logical sequence for there is none)". Only, one might add, the logic of the creative imagination, if it is allowed to grow freely from the first image that shapes itself in the mind.

I have dealt with this matter at some length in my book, *Images of the Dance*, in which I quoted from a number of poets, seeking to isolate a common factor in the creative activities of the poet, choreographer and musician. It is remarkable to see how closely these relate to what George Crumb here writes about his music. For example, T. S. Eliot says: "I know that a poem or a passage of a poem may tend to realize itself first as a particular rhythm before it reaches expression in words, and that this rhythm may bring to birth the idea or the image." This is carried further by the great French poet, Paul Valéry, who writes that his poem "Le Cimetière Marin" sprang "from a rhythmic figure, empty or filled with meaningless symbols which obsessed me for some time". Elsewhere he writes that "known objects and beings are in a way *musicalized*; they have become resonant to each other and as though tuned to our sensibility".

I think what is remarkable in Crumb's music is that these "subliminal images" to which he refers are caught seemingly at his first perception of them; it is like music heard inwardly by the composer, even before he has begun to shape its sound. It is exactly this sense of music rising from the subconscious that has attracted so instinctive a choreographer as Christopher Bruce, who, as we have seen, approaches his work through intuition and not logical planning. In Crumb's music we apprehend the creative act as in some way elemental, when the image rises, whole, alive and with a sudden vividness, as the first light might leap from the hidden sun. The sound we hear is new, strange, created in mysterious sonorities, an attempt to seize the image as it emerges, as distant and evocative as echoes from a dream, lost even at the moment of our waking. It is an inner vision that relates, in its texture and the associations this creates, to the outer world. It is truly elemental, a part of nature; in its distant melodies we hear those that are huge—the movements of the wind and sea; those that are minute—the rustle of an insect's wings. In this, Crumb affords a contrast to music such as Stravinsky's *Rite of Spring*, that seems only self-consciously to achieve this same feeling of elemental power.

George Crumb has written that "music can exist only when the brain is singing", and this seems to me to summarize very exactly what I have been attempting to express. Much avant-garde music appears to lead only to a dead end; one is not conscious of it as belonging to a long tradition, or drawing any inspiration from composers of many different ages and schools. It exists in lonely isolation, remote and unapproachable. George Crumb is, however, very conscious of his inheritance. In the economy and intricacy of his music one can trace the influence of Webern, though Crumb's music gives one a sense of great spaces and wide horizons, while, to me at any rate, Webern is narrow and constricted, drawing away from the outer world with a kind of sour distaste. We find also traces of the ancient plain-song chant in direct quotations from the "Dies Irae" of the Requiem Mass. In his unfamiliar percussive effects one is reminded of the oriental theatre, and the music of the Japanese composer, Toru Takemitsu. His debt to Debussy is, as I have mentioned, particularly great, for both composers are explorers into new lands of tonality and harmony. He has in his work quoted extensively from other composers; from Schubert, where a theme from his quartet, *Death and the Maiden*, is woven into the fabric of one entire section of *Black Angels*; also from Chopin's *Fantasie Impromptu*, a fugue from Bach, Ravel's *Boléro* and Beethoven's *Hammerklavier Sonata*. The scores refer on many occasions to the *Diabolus in Musica*, the tritone, and the Devil's Trill. Although this is by no means an unfamiliar practice with composers, even at times carried to egocentric lengths, as in the manner in which Richard Strauss quotes so extensively from himself, in Crumb's music there is something of the sense of a valediction. He is a man, one feels, deeply conscious of his troubled age; indeed *Black Angels* is an open expression of the composer's anguish over the war in Vietnam, and in his music he appears to look back with regret towards composers of an earlier time.

In his search for new tonal colours and a wider spectrum of sonorities, George Crumb has made use of conventional instruments, either tuned to a higher pitch, electronically projected, or else modified by an unexpected way of playing them. He has incorporated exotic instruments, particularly in the percussion section, and has made his own, almost improvised experiments in ways of obtaining new sound.

This, of course, is no new feature in contemporary music where these experiments have been carried to unusual extremes, so that even the human voice has had its tone altered. In Ligeti's *Aventures*, for example, the singer is directed to block his nose, cover his mouth with his hands and use a megaphone to alter the vocal timbre. In a work by Salvatore Martirano the singer is required to breathe helium, thus causing his voice to sound restricted and high-pitched. In a way this is a return, but fortunately by less drastic methods, to the effects of the *castrati* singers of the eighteenth century whose vocal qualities were so admired by Mozart.

George Crumb is extraordinarily venturesome in this search for new harmonies. Among the unusual instruments he has demanded are water gongs, pitched antique cymbals, musical saws, water-tuned crystal glasses, slide whistles, Chinese prayer stones and Japanese Kabuki blocks. In addition he produces new sonorities by using more conventional instruments in a way which, with a lesser composer, might be considered eccentric, not to say downright absurd. In *Echoes of Time and the River*, for example, at one moment the percussionist lowers and raises a gong in a bucket of water, the score specifying that this should be exactly nine inches deep. Sometimes violinists achieve strange, gossamer-like tones, barely within our hearing, by drawing their bows across the lips of crystal water glasses, each filled to a different level. A steel chain is laid across the piano strings in *Makrokosmos I*, where throughout one movement it eerily jingles. He has even made use of recordings of the sounds made by hump-backed whales in *Voices of the Whale*. In *Ancient Voices of Children* he uses a chisel with a smooth cutting edge, five-eighths of an inch (as indicated in the score), so that this is drawn across the piano strings to produce magical and airy glissandos, as if one could hear the shimmering of the stars. A more chilling effect of rapid tremolos on violin, banjo or piano strings is achieved by touching them with the hands when wearing several thimbles. It is true, at public concerts, such an episode as lowering the gong into a tub of water does produce a certain hilarity among the audience, but the effect for the listener not put under comparable strain is truly magical.

The scores for these works are of incredible beauty and dexterity, forming patterns to relate to the music contained within them. In several works a favourite quotation from Lorca, "the broken arches where time suffers", is indicated on the score by a half-circle or a broken arch. The movement called "Magic Circle of Infinity and Spiral Galaxy" in *Makrokosmos I* is written in circles and the "Crucifixus" is notated in the shape of a cross.

The total effect of these strange compositions is quite astounding. Much of it seems to belong to a world of vast spaces, the huge void of the sky, the movement of an empty sea, the almost inaudible music of the wind, blown it seems from a night of dead stars; or sometimes it is as cold and bleak as the scarred face of the moon. It is silence enclosed by echoes. When I first listened to his music a famous phrase from Pascal's *Pensées* came, suddenly, into my mind: "Le silence éternel des espaces infinis m'effraie"; and it was curious to read some time later how this famous sentence has been one of his main inspirations for *Makrokosmos I*. This is not to attribute myself with exceptional perception, but rather to show the precision and emotional truth of the images George Crumb evokes.

In the same work Crumb tells us how he found inspiration in Rilke's statement, "And in the nights the heavy earth is falling from all the stars down into loneliness. We all are falling. And yet there is one who holds this falling endlessly gently in his hands." This tells us more about the heart of his music than pages of analysis; its deep seriousness, its compassion and its search for truth beyond the reach of our understanding. We hear his music as if from far away, as it reaches us in whispers, in single notes fading, pale and translucent, like those wisps of light around the moon.

Sometimes a single held note will seem to plunge out of the darkness like a comet, or fade slowly like a spent star. Crumb uses many effects whereby a single note increases slowly in volume, thickens, diminishes and falls into silence; or else, by a subtle manipulation of discords, produces a clash of colour, sudden and fierce, like a blaze of light. Other moments have a brilliance that is like the reflection of sun from ice, or like the fire that burns in the heart of a diamond. The music seems to express those thoughts and emotions of ours that are so subtle, so difficult to grasp, always just to the edge where truth is hidden as if behind a shimmering veil.

Often in his music we hear the whisper of ghostly speakers, distant and conspiratorial, abandoned on the edge of silence; then the sudden incantations of strange tongues, as if all humanity cried out in unison, cried to the indifferent stars. We are like eavesdroppers, hearing far voices, lost often in the lamenting wind. There is huge compassion in this music, but one that is unavailing; it can only listen in a great quietness to these cries that are like the bitter call of sea-birds across the wastes of an empty sea. We are aware of the artist listening and watching; in the words of Miguel Unamuno, we are aware of "the tragic sense of life".

A poet whose work has deeply influenced George Crumb is García Lorca, whose tragic death in the Spanish Civil War was so great a loss to European culture. Lorca has written of the artist's sensibility as "a wound that never closes"; and this is highly relevant to Crumb's music, where the composer seems to leave himself open to the sufferings and loneliness of his fellow men.

One can understand how deeply Crumb has been affected by Lorca's poems, not only in the general atmosphere of his music, but in his setting of various poems in *Night Music I*, *Night of the Four Moons* and *Ancient Voices of Children*, to which, in 1975, Christopher Bruce composed his magnificent ballet, itself one of the most remarkable and moving works of the last decade.

In Lorca's poem *La Luna Asoma*, incorporated by Crumb into the structure of *Night Music*, there is one quatrain that is almost a summary of the central obsession of Crumb's works:

Leigh Warren

Bob Smith

Zoltan Imre, Bob Smith

Lucy Burge

Zoltan Imre with group

Zoltan Imre

Sylvia Yamada, Lucy Burge, Zoltan Imre, Catherine Becque

Zoltan Imre, Bob Smith in group

The Music

When the moon rises,
the sea covers the land,
and the heart feels
like an island in infinity.

How close this is to those lonely echoes in his music that
sound what Matthew Arnold called:

... the turbid ebb and flow
Of human misery ...

Earlier in this poem, *Dover Beach*, Arnold writes what one
might describe as a verbal equivalent to the underlying sadness
in Crumb's music, even to its serene acceptance of human
loneliness and the grief in so much of our living:

Listen! you hear the grating roar
Of pebbles which the waves draw back, and fling,
At their return, up the high strand,
Begin, and cease, and then again begin,
With tremulous cadence slow, and bring
The eternal note of sadness in.

There is, however, in Crumb's music no sense of self-pity that
makes certain works of Mahler and Tchaikovsky so distasteful;
for it is a mature understanding of human grief, seen in the wide
span of human history, against the vast perspectives of the sea
and the night sky.

The texture of Lorca's poetry, with its clash of surrealist
images, its wide horizons and sudden outbreaks of violence,
has no parallel in English verse, though it relates very closely to
the poems of Vladimir Mayakovsky in Russian and Guillaume
Apollinaire in French. The nearest equivalent might be Edith
Sitwell's great and now neglected poem, *Gold Coast Customs*.
Certainly it is similar, both in mood and structure, to George
Crumb's music.

It was while Crumb was attending the University of Michigan
that he first became aware of the beauty of the Spanish language
and the poems of Lorca through hearing Lorca's *Casida of the
Boy Wounded by the Water*, set to music by a fellow graduate,
Edward Chudacoff. Although Crumb does not speak Spanish,

the poems of Lorca are the works to which he returns again and again for inspiration. He seems particularly drawn, not only to this sense of loneliness and the pain of human living that is so much a part of Lorca's work, but also to his obsession with death (so common a phenomenon among Spaniards that it is expressed in one word, *duende*) that also holds so central a place in Spanish painting, particularly in that of Goya, and in the ritual sacrifice of the bull-fight. Between its passages of an almost glacial calm, so still that the music seems to be without movement like a motionless sea, there is much anger and violence, particularly in *Black Angels* and also in *Songs, Drones and Refrains of Death*, composed for baritone soloist, with guitar, piano and double bass, the latter based on a cycle of Lorca's poems.

Apart from the poetry of Lorca, other main inspirations for Crumb's work are the complex theories of numerology, also those of astrology (in common with a number of modern composers), and various concepts on the nature of time—an interest shared by many artists in this century, seen particularly in the writings of Bergson and Proust. It is for this reason that Lorca's image of "the broken arches where time suffers" has so particular a significance for Crumb that it is quoted in a number of works. Above all, however, we find this sense of Pascal's "infinite spaces", the loneliness of men lost beneath these "broken arches". Indeed this has been described by one critic as Crumb's "private nightmare" whose fearful obsessions he asks us to share, in those cold spaces beyond the last stars that glimmer so distantly in his music.

We must now turn from these general considerations to *Black Angels* itself. The work is sub-titled "Thirteen Images from the Dark Land", and was composed in 1970 for a string quartet electrically amplified. The composer achieves ghostly effects where the performers play by drawing the bows across the lips of partly-filled water glasses. The musicians are instructed to speak and whisper in various languages including French, German, Russian, Hungarian, Japanese and Swahili (possibly to indicate the universality of the theme of human suffering); at moments they are asked to whistle; also to shake maracas and play *pizzicato* with the same hand. A witty American critic put the matter nicely when he said that "no tone is left unturned".

Yet *Black Angels* is a profoundly serious work, dealing with the ultimate struggle of good and evil, the dark and light, which is the primary symbol of art. It is savage, despairing, filled with a sense of brutal conflict which is never finally resolved, as, indeed, it never is in our mortal world. The Black Angels, the bringers of evil and death, are, of course, based on the myth of the fall of Lucifer and the angels from heaven—the first and most terrible of all rebellions against God. They are the bringers of war, famine and death, made more terrible by the nature of their fall, for they were the chosen ones of God. As Shakespeare tells us in one immortal sentence: "Angels are bright although the brightest fell."

As Crumb has drawn upon the works of Rilke for his inspiration in *Night Music I*, composed seven years before *Black Angels*, he is certain to be aware of the famous opening to the *Duineser Elegien*:

> Who, if I cried, would hear me among the angelic orders?

One feels this lament is contained in the music with the same poignancy, the same despairing beauty. It is true, of course, that Rilke was not invoking the angels of theology, but rather those of the imagination, but Crumb's music uses angels in a somewhat similar way to describe the nightmare that haunts his mind. Our response to the music must be a personal one, since like all great works it exists on many different levels, and is rich, like the finest poetry, in many hidden associations. I have written this chapter before Christopher Bruce began work on his ballet, and the reader as well as myself is to discover into what regions the choreographer's vision of the music is to lead him. They will certainly be different from my own, for they will be his own insight, his own discovery of Crumb's dark land. In giving below my own impressions of the music, I am not disturbed by the thought that the choreographer may see it differently, for there are many angles from which one can look at the stars.

Black Angels is based on a complex numerological formula

involving the figures seven and thirteen. The number seven was considered by the Babylonians, Persians and Greeks to be a sacred number. As they believed that astronomy was the basis for religion, they divided the firmament into seven heavens, one for each of the planets. Each of these spheres was ruled by one god, whose ruling power was transferred from one planet to another every tenth day by winged messengers. For that reason temples, towers and ziggurats were built in seven storeys, and it is thought that the Tower of Babel was such a structure. It is interesting that Glen Tetley composed his remarkable ballet, performed by Ballet Rambert, *Ziggurat*, clearly based on the same numerological formula.

I think it is important in the understanding of Crumb's music to realize how much of it is based on the ideas of the pre-Christian philosophers and astrologers. His world of star-lit empty spaces, the blowing of distant winds, the hollow echoes in the void through which they move is, in my view, an attempt to express the primal source of music as it was discerned by these philosophers. The Pythagoran belief that there was a correlation between the ratios of musical intervals and the ratios of the orbits of celestial bodies, in which each sphere is guided by a siren singing one tone of the musical scale, was incorporated by Plato into his *Republic* to describe how all creation moved in harmony in a kind of celestial dance. The sirens were, like the winged messengers of earlier civilizations, taken over into Christian theology in the form of angels, and this was a concept easily understood in times distant from our own. It was clearly accepted by Shakespeare where, in a famous passage at the end of *The Merchant of Venice*, Lorenzo says to Jessica:

> . . . Look how the floor of heaven
> Is thick inlaid with patines of bright gold:
> There's not the smallest orb which thou behold'st
> But in his motion like an angel sings,
> Still quiring to the young-eyed cherubims;
> Such harmony is in immortal souls . . .

Plato describes heaven as a huge globe, ringed by a shining band similar to the rainbow. Running from this is a spindle, attached to which are eight discs of different colours; on the edge of each a siren sits, singing one note of the musical scale. The spindle is kept moving by three Fates—past, present and future. The soul moves in the air around the spindle. The sirens make the music of immortal spheres, expressing the Divine harmony of the universe.

Dionysius had established the order of the angelic choirs (one notes again the musical association) which was incorporated into Christian theology. Writing in the fourth century, Tertullian says "Every spirit is winged, so it is with angels, so it is with devils". Such beings are a very ancient concept of mankind, whose traces can still be found today. In the British Museum there is a relief from the Tomb of the Harpies near the Lycian town of Xanthos that shows a number of winged creatures, half woman, half bird, leading the spirits of the dead to another world. Winged beings are also shown on Assyrian reliefs, guarding the tree of life and in those of the Hittites as guardians of the sun god. Dancing angels appear frequently in Christian iconography from the first half of the fourteenth century, and they are seen in Fra Angelico's two paintings of the Last Judgement as well as in his great work, "The Death and Assumption of the Virgin". They also occur in Botticelli's illustrations to Dante's *Paradiso*. In many pictures from this period onwards, angels are depicted as carrying musical instruments: in many cases, both for the evil harpies and the Christian angels, they are seen as women.

Black Angels are those who rebelled against God and were flung from heaven by the angel Michael; as we are told in the *Book of Revelation*: "Michael and the angels fought with the dragon and the dragon fought all his angels, and they prevailed not, nor was their place found any more in heaven".

They have been for centuries in Christian theology considered to be the bringers of evil and death to the world; so that the Dance of Death—one of the most prevalent symbols in music and painting since the great bubonic plagues of the fourteenth century—and the Angel of Death have never been far from the consciousness of artists, returning in every century (as they return in Crumb's music for *Black Angels*) and in many different guises. They differ from the angels of whom we read in the *Apocalypse*, who deliver the seven vessels of God's wrath to mankind; for the Black Angels bring evil to the world, not as retribution, but in an effort to shatter the harmony of God's creation, shaped in the logic of music and the song of the immortal spheres.

The music of *Black Angels* is divided into thirteen sections, as follows: 1) *Departure:* (i) Threnody I: Night of the Electric Insects, (ii) Sounds of bones and flutes, (iii) Lost Bells, (iv) Devil-music, (v) Danse Macabre; 2) *Absence:* (vi) Pavane Lachrymae (der Tod und das Mädchen), (vii) Threnody II: Black Angels, (viii) Sarabanda de la Muerte Oscura, (ix) Lost Bells (Echo); 3) *Return:* (x) God-music, (xi) Ancient Voices, (xii) Ancient Voices (Echo), (xiii) Threnody III: Night of the Electric Insects.

It will be seen that the pattern, Departure, Absence and Return, follows the same structure as Beethoven's piano sonata No. 26 in E flat, Op. 81a (Les Adieux); and there are moments in which the sense of nostalgia and the loneliness of abandonment in Beethoven's great work are very closely echoed. Further classical references are to a theme from Schubert's Quartet, *Death and the Maiden*, upon which a considerable part of section (vi) is based. References are also made to the "Dies Irae" of the plain-chant Requiem Mass mainly in section (iv).

Although the work abounds in extra-musical references and could indeed be considered as "programme music", it would be invidious for me, in advance of the choreographer, to set any dramatic pattern to the whole design; my concern, in describing the work, is to indicate its structure and the various emotional possibilities latent in each section. Indeed the fascination for myself and (I hope) the reader lies in the fact that, as I write this, I have no idea how the choreographer is going to treat the music, whose images are at the moment hidden in the secrecy of his own mind.

The first section of *Black Angels*, "Night of the Electric Insects", opens in a shrill cry from the whole quartet, at once anguished and yet full of menace; it throbs in the air like the hugely-magnified sound of insects' wings scraping, harsh and dry, against one another. They come nearer, fade into the distance, then return. One thinks of a cloud of gnats swirling in the darkness: surely indeed these are the black angels, the enraged cry of the damned spirits as they fall from heaven. Or one is reminded of the devils who appeared to St Teresa of Avila like innumerable insects that she had to frighten away with blows from her prayer book. Between their music is heard a plaintive cry, almost like the mewing of a cat, a kind of anguished appeal. Then the insects disappear, and one is reminded (remembering that this music was written during the war in Vietnam) of a flight of aircraft, their hideous mission accomplished, disappearing over the horizon.

There follows the section, "Sounds of bones and flutes", full of grotesque humour. We hear the dance of the bones, the aimless jigging of the skeleton through whom the wind seems to ventriloquize, speaks with the gaping mouth, explores the sockets of the skull, makes the empty nostrils for a moment breathe again. It is as if the bones rose up, shaping as they do so the human frame; in the music we can hear the click of bone on bone. The parallel to the famous section of the *Book of Ezekiel* is very close:

> So I prophesied as I was commanded: and as I prophesied, there was a noise and behold a shaking, and the bones came together, bone to his bone. And when I beheld, lo, the sinews and the flesh came up upon them, and the skin covered them above; but there was no breath in them.

This passage has been transposed in section two of T. S. Eliot's *Ash Wednesday*, with which I am sure the composer is familiar; maybe indeed these two passages were in his mind as he evoked the hollow rattle of the dancing bones.

> . . . And God said
> Prophesy to the wind, to the wind only for only
> The wind will listen. And the bones sang chirping
> With the burden of the grasshopper . . .

The introduction of flute-like music here is marvellously appropriate, since a flute is the nearest instrument to a bone and gives us the sound of the wind reaching within the skull, prying through the sockets of the eyes. An echo from Rilke, the third

Elegy, reaches us in this music: "Hark how the night grows fluted and hollowed".

This is the first section of dance in the music, in which one seems to watch the grotesque lolling of the skull, a strange gavotte of skeletons dancing in the wind.

The third section, "Lost Bells", is choral, almost organ-like, in which we hear the distant tolling of bells with that hollow sound of music carried over water. At the beginning of this section we are introduced to their chiming, but when they return it is a single tolling, like that of a passing bell. Once again we hear the pathetic mewing sound, and this is transformed into a glimpse of the plain-chant "Dies Irae", the lament of the dead.

Here the great sadness of the music—the dance of the bones, the clamour of distant bells—has the same tragic urgency as these lines from Eliot's *The Dry Salvages*:

> There is no end of it, the voiceless wailing,
> No end to the withering of withered flowers,
> To the movement of pain that is painless and motionless,
> To the drift of the sea and the drifting wreckage,
> The bone's prayer to Death its God . . .

The fourth and fifth sections are the most sinister of the whole work in which several elements, hinted at in the earlier parts, now come together—the scream of the insects; the sound of the "Dies Irae", now thickened by heavy string tone, and, later, savagely distorted; the plaintive cry we heard in the first section of the music. Between these there are cadenza-like passages in which we seem to watch the dance of the Angel of Death himself. The "Dance Macabre" is heavily rhythmic, to a stamping rhythm in which there are hints of the dance of the bones, as if they too joined in this terrible festival. The music concludes with the sound of human voices, a jagged end to this fearsome dance whose rhythm pervades the silence when the voices cease.

The second part of *Black Angels* opens with a beautiful restatement of the theme from the *andante* of Schubert's quartet, *Death and the Maiden*. It is like a funeral procession, whose silence is broken only by the lamenting winds, though, high above, we catch the sound of the insect voices, as if they watched over a world of human misery they had created. At the end the theme is broken by the whining of the wind, come darkly from the void, the chaos beyond the last stars.

The black angels return in the following threnody, their fierce and impetuous flight like that of Shelley's autumn leaves: "like ghosts from an enchanter fleeing".

There are echoes of the earlier "Danse Macabre" but here the tone is more frenzied, whipped on by voices full of urgency, even of command. It is one of the most furious sections of the music, a restless dance, full of a sense not only of menace but of a deep inner restlessness and dissatisfaction. If indeed these are the voices of the black angels, one feels that they come to torment mankind only because they are themselves so cruelly tormented.

The Sarabande that follows opens again to the sound of the insects caught within the wind. This leads to a tune of deep melancholy, round which, as in the section "Death and the Maiden", the insect voices hover in menacing descant. It is a melody even more grief-stricken than the earlier one, since it seems without purpose or sense of any sort of finality; men will grieve so, one thinks, until the end of time. This section ends with the theme of the "Dies Irae" sounded, high and shrill, on the insect voices.

We return, in section nine, to the lost bells of the first part, dominated by the "Dies Irae" and the ghostly dance of the bones in the earlier sections of the music. This concludes the second part, wherein the tone has been as despairing as any I know in music—the chaos of our cruel age caught in a moment of nightmare, a vision of a waste land as terrible, yet so similar in its imagery, as that evoked by Eliot half a century before, when he writes:

> What is that sound high in the air
> Murmur of maternal lamentation
> Who are those hooded hordes swarming
> Over endless plains, stumbling in cracked earth
> Ringed by the flat horizon only
> What is the city over the mountains
> Cracks and reforms and bursts in the violet air

The Music

> Falling towers
> Jerusalem Athens Alexandria
> Vienna London
> Unreal

One cannot but feel that this section of *The Waste Land*, incorporating as it does the images of evil, winged creatures, bells and the bone, cannot have been far from consciousness when the composer sought for his inspiration. One has only to note how the poem continues after the passage I have just quoted:

> A woman drew her long black hair out tight
> And fiddled whisper music on those strings
> And bats with baby faces in the violet light
> Whistled, and beat their wings
> And crawled head downward down a blackened wall
> And upside down in air were towers
> Tolling reminiscent bells, that kept the hours
> And voices singing out of empty cisterns and exhausted wells.
>
> In this decayed hole among the mountains
> In the faint moonlight, the grass is singing
> Over the tumbled graves, about the chapel
> There is the empty chapel, only the wind's home.
> It has no windows, and the door swings,
> Dry bones can harm no one.

The composer who has in his music explored what he describes as Images from the Dark Land is not far from the poet; for each, their anguished imagination is seen in terms of the collapse of the social order. I do not think one should underestimate the effect of the war in Vietnam upon the American conscience; it has seared the imagery of many of its finest poets, threatened, as they saw it, with moral anarchy in exactly the same manner as Eliot observed the collapse of traditional values in the period after the first world war. Further, *The Waste Land* had marked indelibly the consciousness of all artists of George Crumb's generation and my own; its imagery is part of one's unconscious life.

The third and final section of *Black Angels* opens with what

71

the composer describes as "God-music". Here on a long flowing melody, almost Brahmsian in shape, we discover peace—a peace that has been sought for, longed for, the wide serenity of all immortal music. It is of quite extraordinary beauty, almost mystical in its intensity, like the *adagios* from Beethoven's last string quartets. After the anguish of the earlier music, with its brutal rhythms and harsh broken lines, this section is an invocation of an eternal repose, the peace that we are told passes all understanding. It opens with the sound as of a harmonica, strange distant music like the shimmer of light around the stars, and from this the great tune begins, glows in mysterious beauty like the light from the rising sun. This is Plato's music of the spheres, the siren voices singing from the far stars, to whose great harmony the whole of creation moves as in a dance. The sublime music fades on thin notes almost beyond our hearing, and lingers through the following two sections called "Ancient Voices".

Played mainly in irregular *pizzicato* these sections are like a conversation between two people, full of tentative questions, words that hang uneasily over a void of silence, or break on a note of interrogation as if to ask of those wide stars from which the celestial music came, "why should this be so, why should it be?" The black angels return, coupled with those menacing voices that seem to shout their commands even from the depths of hell.

Slowly the music softens; the voices of the black angels are transformed into a tune on plucked strings that sounds like those of mandolins, now warmer, more human, even at times quietly rejoicing, as if the victory had been won, the ancient struggle between light and darkness at last resolved. But the cry of the wind returns, the scream of the angels on the edge of darkness. Now the music closes, as if it interrogated this darkness, to leave an unanswered question floating on the air. Seven single notes, like the striking of a clock, reach out from this silence as the music ends.

On an empty stage, haunted by the music, the choreographer and his dancers now begin their own journey to this dark land.

4. The Design and Lighting

While it is true that the Diaghilev Ballet brought about a radical new approach to design, rejecting as it did the ideas of a meticulous naturalism that had dominated the past, it also created an imbalance by relegating the dance to a position even at times subservient to the design. It was primarily a painters' theatre, and not that of the dancer; as the great critic, André Levinson, was alone in pointing out, it betrayed the traditions of the classical dance in search of novelty in decoration. From these false aesthetics arose the idea that ballet was an equal partnership of music, design and dance which so dominated the criticism of ballet, to the detriment of the art, in the period after Diaghilev.

Many of these designs, commissioned from the greatest painters of the time, were extremely beautiful, but they concealed from the audience both the poverty of much of the choreography and the distortions of the classical dance. Seen today, ballets such as *Petrushka*, *The Firebird* and *Scheherazade* are lamentably thin in choreographic invention, yet the sets of Benois, Golovine and Bakst remain magnificent examples of theatre decoration. What choreography there was had been entirely swamped by the *décor*; from the point of view of the dance, it was only the presence of great artists such as Nijinsky and Karsavina that brought to these ballets a kind of dazzling individual brilliance which has not survived. This increasingly dominant position given to the design reached its climax in Massine's ballet, *Parade*, a witless and jejune fabrication, completely swamped by Picasso's extraordinary cubist *décor* and costumes which were so cumbersome, so disproportioned, that the dancers could barely move in them let alone perform the choreography, little enough though there was.

This is not to deny that there were magnificent exceptions where the choreographer demanded a simplicity in line that did not swamp his work. Marie Laurencin's design for *Les Biches* and the stark simplicity of Natalia Goncharova's sets for *Les Noces* are superb works that enhance the choreography, but only because Nijinska insisted on clear, simple lines and rejected the opulent costumes Diaghilev first suggested for *Les Noces*. In the same way, Picasso's designs for *The Three-*

77

Cornered Hat achieved a perfect setting for Massine's superb choreography, in fine contrast to Derain's pretty but cluttered backdrop for *La Boutique Fantasque*.

Perhaps the greatest designer to emerge in the post-Diaghilev period was Christian Bérard whose wonderful sets for Balanchine's *Cotillon* and Massine's *Seventh Symphony* gave the choreographer a perfect, uncluttered backcloth on which to work, beautiful in the clarity of its line and the elegance of its proportions. Bérard was the guiding spirit of Roland Petit's remarkable company *Les Ballets des Champs Elysées*, the first to visit London after the war, and his magnificent sets for *Les Forains*, and, later, *La Rencontre*, set a standard in modern ballet design which has rarely been equalled.

Roland Petit was also to bring us *décors* by Clavé, Carzou and Wakhevitch which combined a dazzling simplicity with a compression of imagery that were among the wonders of the post-war theatre. I recall few excitements in the ballet greater than the first glimpse of Clavé's sets for Roland Petit's *Carmen*, a series of seemingly disconnected props—a red curtain, an old bed, a birdcage and a cartwheel that turned slowly on a rope—that encapsulated the whole drama in a series of unforgettable images.

It was this economy, the setting of brilliant detail and simplicity of line, that was also found in the work of Sophie Fedorovitch, which pointed towards the future. Fedorovitch was undoubtedly the greatest designer produced during the pre-war years of ballet in this country. Her sets for *Les Masques*, *Symphonic Variations*, *La Fête Etrange* and *Veneziana* were miracles of design, where the simplicity was to shimmer within a misty opalescence of extraordinary beauty.

Fedorovitch worked directly from models and on the dancers; her sets were not a vastly-expanded painting like so many of the Diaghilev period. The stage was no longer cluttered with unnecessary detail, the lines of the choreography and the figures of the dancers, *seen in movement*, were never obstructed or distracted by the sets. She designed for dancing, and her sets and costumes enhanced the choreography. It is, perhaps, significant that her finest work, for Ashton's *Symphonic*

Variations, was in a ballet that affirmed uncompromisingly the primacy of the dance against the false aesthetics of the past, immured in Fokine's famous five principles, and the theories about the dance that had resulted from them which were now seen to have no real validity.

The primacy of the dance has, of course, been even more strongly affirmed by Balanchine, particularly in those works created for New York City Ballet. He has, in fact, more or less dismissed the designer, preferring that his ballets should be danced in practice dress against a neutral background. I find his later work to be cold, empty and sterile, but there is no doubt that it has buried the aesthetics of the Diaghilev Ballet for a long time to come.

It is against this brief sketch of the development of design in ballet that one must see the works of present-day artists, of whom one of the most distinguished is Nadine Baylis. They seek for the same kind of compression of images and simplicity of line achieved by the greatest of their predecessors, notably Clavé and Fedorovitch. This is not only a matter of aesthetics, but also one of simple economics. Elaborate stage settings, except for the few great national companies remaining, are now financially impossible; also the companies with which these designers work perform on a variety of different stages, different not only in size but also in relationship to the audience. Ballet Rambert, for whom Nadine Baylis has designed so many ballets, works not only in small university and civic theatres, but also in the round and in very close proximity to the audience in such theatres as the Young Vic and the Roundhouse. The Company is on tour for at least thirty weeks of the year; for this reason elaborate sets would be entirely impracticable, as well as quite unsuitable for the type of ballets in which it performs.

It is also true, I think, that the influence of the so-called modern dance companies from the United States, particularly those of Martha Graham and Alwin Nikolais, has led to this almost epigrammatic simplicity of most modern ballet design. A number of sets for Martha Graham's company were designed by Isamu Noguchi where clarity, compression and symbolic meaning have become prime considerations. In the same manner, the brilliant lighting effects achieved for New York City Ballet by Jean Rosenthal have led designers to establish their work in a far more three-dimensional manner, where lighting and shadow are of prime importance, in a way the easel painters of the past, however brilliant, would not have considered.

From the moment she was first taken to the theatre at the age of fourteen, Nadine Baylis has never wanted to be anything else but a designer; surprisingly, and unlike most children, she never dreamed of being either an actress or a dancer, but at once saw her destiny and followed it. She was trained at the Central School of Art in London, and gained practical understanding of the theatre from a period with the Royal Shakespeare Company at Stratford. She feels that the greatest influences upon her from that time were John Berry and Ralph Koltai, from whom she assimilated the many new ideas of design that had a kind of Brechtian severity and clarity of purpose now found in her own work.

Although she has worked for many different companies, including the Royal Ballet, Festival Ballet, the Stuttgart Ballet and the Australian Ballet, so that she is now one of the most sought-after designers in the theatre, her first love is Ballet Rambert. She has been associated particularly with three choreographers—Glen Tetley, Norman Morrice and Christopher Bruce, for whose ballets she has the most profound admiration and with whom she works in the closest harmony. Among the ballets she has designed for Christopher Bruce have been *Ancient Voices of Children, Duets, There Was a Time, Living Space* and *Unfamiliar Playground.*

Her starting point, she tells me, is the dance image; and part of her admiration for these three choreographers stems from the fact that they work in terms of images rather than steps. She can admire choreographers who compose largely through variations on the academic technique, but her inspiration comes mainly from the image, creating a world which she describes as a new language. "It becomes" (she says) "a shared experience between the audience and the dancers, as if you were suddenly able to speak a new language, to enter a dream-world of images. And it is their strange ambiguity, the world of associations that they bring with them, that is the most powerful influence on me as a designer." It is her greatest concern and principal anxiety that her designs do not in any way either too greatly reinforce or distort the images the choreographer has envisaged. "You must be true to his vision and to your own."

Nadine Baylis agrees that the ballet was for a very long period—so long in fact that it became a tradition—too much under the influence of the painter, whose designs, brilliant or original as they may be, rarely work in the theatre. This tradition, she feels, has done great harm both to the ballet and to the painters, but it is one that has now been overtaken by new ideas in which a far greater economy and clarity of effect have been achieved.

The first concern of the designer, she believes, is to show off the choreography to its greatest advantage, and to allow the dancers space and freedom in which to work. One has only to consider how much these two ideals have been disregarded in the past to realize how new a concept it is. Many artists, particularly painters, have cramped the dancers and swamped the choreography through too strident an insistence upon their own vision. A cursory glance through Cyril Beaumont's book, *Ballet Design: Past and Present*, is enough to confirm this. Even the most famous sets, like those of Léon Bakst for *The Good-humoured Ladies*, brutally mistreat the dancers by cramping them into such small confines, while so many other designs, as, for example, Leslie Hurry's sets for Robert Helpmann's *Hamlet*, completely overpower the choreography, and, worse still, distort the images of the created dance. If in a review one reads a great deal about the design, it seems to me that it has failed. Nor do such excesses belong to the past: the sets for many modern productions swamp the choreography by this crowding of detail.

Nadine Baylis maintains that the designer should work from the beginning in three-dimensional images, seeing the dancer in sculptural terms, in her own words "as a figure in space". For this reason she prefers to work from models for the set and directly on the dancer for costumes. It does not seem to her right that the dancers should "be forced to cope with some alien garments which have been designed without consulting them and which they will probably not wear until the dress rehearsal. I don't like costumes which are like pieces of sculpture the dancers have to carry around, extraneous to the way they move in that particular ballet, as if some sort of idea had been grafted on to them."

It is for this reason that she does not like to begin work on the set and costumes until the choreography is completed, and she has gained a deep understanding of this by watching it during the process of creation. She must understand its language, know the particular images she has to answer in her designs and the quality of the movement of the dancers, before she feels free to begin to create. This ideal is more easy to achieve in a small company like Ballet Rambert, where workshop facilities are on the premises and the tradition of a close co-operation between all those taking part in the ballet is accepted. She will then be able to choose the materials, cut the costumes herself, and, if necessary, make them up, consulting the dancer at each stage to see that he or she is at ease within them.

Her belief that the dancers must have the greatest possible space in which to move, accentuated in the case of Ballet Rambert who work for considerable periods on the tiny stage of the Jeannetta Cochrane Theatre, means the closest possible co-operation with the workshop staff and the lighting designer. "We are" (she says) "a kind of Mafia, always in a mysterious huddle together." Perspective masking of the stage must be avoided, and this causes new problems in lighting, since the lights have to be placed further back, thus affecting their "throw".

Nadine Baylis grew up in the theatre at a time when many new materials became available, as well as ideas in the use of metal and plastic instead of canvas and paint. The metal framework she set around the dancers in Christopher Bruce's *Unfamiliar Playground*, where they seemed to move within a cage of frozen air, is a fine example of her imaginative use of metal structures. And she does not believe that the actual structure of the set should, of necessity, be hidden, for it may be beautiful in its own right. "The Unit is in fact beautiful in itself—that is, an inevitable piece of design and not a perverting of its nature; you allow it to take its natural strength."

Sets seen thus in three dimensions, whether they are constructional or in a more formal design, "allow the choreographer a hard line to set a soft line against". This, Nadine Baylis feels, is rather the same principle of the musical stave which exists to bring up the written notes with the greatest clarity. Modern choreographers like Tetley and Christopher Bruce are most concerned with pure lines, so that nothing in the costumes or the sets must impede this; all must be stripped bare, so that the dance is sharply etched. Further, the design must light well. "I allow in creating it," Nadine Baylis says, "something to be added there by the light."

One of her most important concerns is not to stress any particular element of the choreography or music to the extent that it might affect the balance of the whole. Here it is necessary to be ruthless with oneself, and sometimes she has scrapped completed sets altogether, or rejected costumes, if she finds anything within them that seems to encroach on the choreographer's vision, or emphasizes one certain aspect of it too definitely. "One must be prepared to be ruthless" (she says) "with others if necessary as well as with oneself." The great danger is that one becomes too attached to a certain image, to a favourite way of seeing. This idea is central to her artistic belief. "You must be prepared to throw away the things to which you are most attached, both in art and life; by their very intensity and your concern for them they restrict your vision beyond them. One must not feel there is anything sacred among one's ideas."

Nadine Baylis greatly admires choreographers for their ability to discard a favourite image if it does not fit into the totality of the design or the music. "Christopher Bruce is brutal with himself; he is never self-indulgent. He is one of the most direct and honest choreographers I have ever worked with." In this respect she feels that choreographers differ from theatrical directors who often cling to those "sacred and tender moments"

of a production, even at the expense of the balance and coherence of the whole.

The vision she will create to free the choreography and the music will be her own; it will, as she describes it, "walk hand in hand with the choreography". It has been her experience with young choreographers composing their first works that they are inclined to give too precise instructions on what design they require and thus weaken the impact of their choreography. Design, she maintains, must be an original vision that harmonizes with their own, but it is a different aspect of the same truth. Choreography, the design and music are three different, though related, dimensions within which the work of art exists.

Nadine Baylis finds that sometimes with very complex movement one has to strip the design almost bare, so that it is a kind of "negation of design". This was the case with her sets for *Ancient Voices of Children* where the dance images seemed to echo those of Goya, particularly in the *Capricios*, so that she felt she must provide designs that would be not another dimension but "a kind of shadow, hinting only at the themes of poverty and richness, only half there and only partly stated".

Another serious problem, often ignored by ballet designers, is that certain movements or images will not carry in the theatre in the same way as they do in the dance studio, where the choreographer is working a short distance away from the dancers. It is the task of the designer to visualize how these images will appear from the audience, many of whom will be far from the stage. She will have to project them, make them carry the distance. It is therefore often necessary to scrap or ignore images that do not project except at close quarters, though some will be there, and indeed must be there within the choreography and the design, even if the audience does not see them.

There is a great deal of practicality and theatrical common sense in Nadine Baylis' ideas as a designer. She has a detailed knowledge of different materials, knows how they will look in the light, how they will fall or shape a movement, right down to such practical details as to what materials you cannot use because of fire regulations. She is fascinated by the mechanics of stage setting, the different kinds of structure and the metals that

85

can be used. She has studied the effects of optical illusion and its uses in the theatre. She understands lighting, and has, in fact, lit one of her own sets in Germany when no lighting designer was available. Yet, behind this kind of craftmanship and professional expertise, there is a visionary who seeks beyond the music and beyond the dance for their secret imagery which is her love and the inspiration of her art.

It was Christopher Bruce's early intention that the sets should be done in advance of the choreography, but she never really trusts herself to work in this manner. A ballet, in her view, is set on the edge of perilous extremities, "a frightening confrontation between the choreographer, the dancers and the music" from which the images of the dance are wrested. She and Bruce thus decided to wait until the choreography was completed, as neither of them was truly satisfied with their first concepts of the theme and the music. In fact Christopher Bruce was to make a radical alteration to the theme and the structure only when he was near the end of the choreography.

When I discussed these matters with her, some four weeks before the first performance, Nadine Baylis had completed and then abandoned one concept of the design. At first she had felt that the religious symbolism of the ballet should be indicated in the design, but later changed her mind, so that it was not until the model was virtually complete that she had a sudden conviction that she had been wrong to omit it. For that reason she decided to start again, despite the amiable mockery of her friends in the Company.

The choreography of *Black Angels* has for her the marvellous simplicity of an icon, an innocence of concept combined with an extreme sophistication in form that reminds her of the work of William Blake. "You do really meet the hand of God." To incorporate this vision, at once so simple and so complex, surrealistic in its presentation, is a new challenge for her; it is yet another language she has suddenly, and as if by magic, learned.

With Ballet Rambert she has found a Company that shares her own sense of dedication and the feeling that every work is a new adventure, a perilous journey into the unknown, in which everyone from the seamstress to the choreographer is involved. "There is", Nadine Baylis told me, "every good reason for the Rambert not existing at all. And this is the best possible way for a Company to exist; in other words, not to be established, be actually at risk." After fifty years the Rambert is still a group of pioneers, and that they have won the affection and admiration of so brilliant a designer is another proof of the seriousness of their endeavour.

Nadine Baylis has worked on many ballets with John B. Read, the lighting designer. They first collaborated on Glen Tetley's *Ziggurat*, and since that time they have been involved in some dozen productions together. They have a very close understanding of each other's ideas which are indeed based on many of the same concepts in relation to the ballet as a whole.

It is only in fairly recent years that lighting design has become an important feature of the theatre; previously it had been left to the director and the chief electrician to settle it between themselves as a somewhat minor aspect of the production. In the same way, during the period of the Diaghilev Ballet, when Diaghilev himself was asked by ill-informed journalists what was his job within the company, he used to reply that he looked after the lighting, as if this were a very humble activity indeed.

However, the brilliant experiments conducted by Jean Rosenthal for New York City Ballet made choreographers aware of the importance of lighting design, and it is this quite new tradition that is now carried on by John B. Read who is probably the most distinguished lighting designer in modern ballet.

Like Nadine Baylis he became aware of his craft at a very early age, and it was in order to become a lighting designer that he joined the Rose Bruford College of Speech and Drama to study its techniques in relationship to those of the drama as a whole. After a three-year course, he took up an appointment with the Mermaid Theatre in 1959 as an electrician, since at that time there were no specialized appointments in lighting design with theatre companies. He then went to the Chichester Festival Theatre when this was opened under the direction of

Sir Laurence Olivier, and it was here that he lit his first work—Peter Shaffer's play, *The Royal Hunt of the Sun*, later to be transferred to the National Theatre at the Old Vic.

This was, he tells me, a disastrous first production from his own point of view, since he was so inexperienced, but his talent was recognized, so that he joined Theatre Projects as a junior designer. Now, however, he works on a free-lance basis. In 1964, when he was working on a production of *As You Like It* at the Old Vic, he was invited by Ralph Koltai to light a ballet for the Rambert Company. Although this was, in fact, postponed, he was later engaged to light the Tetley ballet with sets by Nadine Baylis. Since then he has created lighting designs for all the main ballet companies both in Britain and abroad, including the Royal Ballet, the Festival Ballet, the Stuttgart Ballet, the Scottish Ballet and the London Contemporary Dance Theatre.

As lighting design is such a young art, John Read has had to work out his own procedures, and these are now adapted to all ballet productions for which he is engaged. First he has discussions with the designer regarding the style of the work and the initial ideas for the *décor*, after which he studies the completed choreography in the studio and talks with the choreographer to ascertain from him the quality and type of movement, also those aspects of it that he wishes to be accentuated. As he watches the run-through of the completed ballet he times his probable lighting cues with a stop-watch. In order to obtain what for him will be a kind of working score of the ballet, he draws up sheets of paper into ten squares, on each of which he notes the position of the dancers, synchronized with the running time at each point, together with the lighting effects he is to use. These he indicates by his own symbols—arrows, little squiggles, lines—to represent both the angle and the quality of the lighting.

At this point he works in black and white, more concerned to explore his own feelings regarding the ballet, and he will add colour at a later stage in much the same manner as a composer will orchestrate the skeleton score. He will study the designer's model, probably photograph it, as well as key moments during the ballet, so that he will be able to construct a detailed plan.

From this he will compose the lighting in the theatre, where he is obliged to work very fast, enclosed not only within the time span of the ballet, but also by the limited rehearsal periods available for lighting a production.

After completing his "score" he will have a long discussion with the choreographer over each section of the ballet to ascertain the quality of feeling required within it. On an average there will be about one lighting cue per minute, though this of course varies with the level of emotion within the ballet. A work such as Tetley's *Moveable Garden*, which is on an even, rather quiet emotional key, although longer than *Black Angels*, in fact required far fewer lighting cues—12 against the 24 for *Black Angels*.

Describing the quality of lighting for each individual scene, John Read told me that he felt that it would need a considerable amount of "hot" colours—orange, yellows and greens—while certain sections must look "like slabs of marble"; others again to appear "totally pure" or else suggest "the barren spaces of a waste land". The music is of considerable help to him, not only in suggesting the quality of the lighting, but also in clarifying the intentions of the choreographer if these cannot be fully explained. As I had found, it is difficult for a choreographer to put into words the ideas he expresses in the dance; he is too close to the ballet, too emotionally involved, working from instinct and intuition rather than close logical analysis.

All the preliminary work completed, his lighting cues set, the quality and angles of the lights determined, John Read comes to the theatre with the whole pattern of his design clear in his mind. You must work then, he told me, "as if you had a brush in your hand". Here he will use his intuition, catching hold of some new and unexpected effect of light, either to incorporate it into the design at that moment, or to hold it in reserve for a later section of the ballet. John Read put this to me very succinctly:

If I see something on the stage which I hadn't expected to happen, I'll use it, I'll conjure with it, while not losing control of the built-in plan. These sudden insights when you see a colour behaving in a certain way on people and on faces, you retain in

89

your memory to use later on. You must not disturb the eye with cues that are too fast, those that are too dramatic or out of context, nor must you hinder in any way the total design and the rhythm of the ballet as a whole. You destroy the work of both the choreographer and the dancers if you do that.

John Read then said something that should be written in huge letters at the entrance to every ballet studio, which composers, designers and lighting designers with ideas of their own self-importance, could read each time they enter. "The dancers are the most important designs on the stage, bigger than the sets, bigger than the lighting."

It would be easy for him to stun the audience with brilliant effects, and sacrifice the choreography to his own expertise, but he will never do that any more than will Nadine Baylis. They have the true humility of every artist to the work; their skills are placed at the service of the choreography and the dancers. With real artists in the theatre there is always found this rare quality—a search for the truth of the work and a concern to express this to the greatest advantage: in this they are at one with the dancers, for whom both Nadine Baylis and John Read have so profound a respect.

The set,[1] as it was finally evolved by Nadine Baylis, carried many images, a multiplicity of design entirely at one with the choreography. A huge curved tent in black gauze reached above the dancers, imprisoning them within their own eternity. Inspired by drawings made by many artists to illustrate Dante's *Divine Comedy*, it was also influenced by the water-colour paintings of William Blake. Yet it was her vision, drawn from deep within her unconscious life, giving the sense of an enclosed world set in the cold and empty spaces beyond the stars, around which, in the music, one heard the whine of the icy wind.

It was designed in curves since, Nadine Baylis told me, this is how man envisages the universe and symbolizes eternity, again

[1] Although the *décor* was created after Christopher Bruce had finished the choreography, I have thought it best to place a description of it here, rather than in chronological order, since it grew from many of the ideas Nadine Baylis expressed to me when first discussing the design.

taking up images contained both in the choreography and the music. She saw it as a strange web, like a spider's web, hanging in space. "It is" (she said) "as if the air had solidified." This gave her the idea of a texture that would be fragile, yet could not be broken, a design that "has its own perfection and cuts through the air". This hell is limitless as the damned see it, frail as gossamer, yet enclosing them utterly, of such immense strength for all its seeming fragility that it can never be broken. Suspended in the air, it is curved like the wings of some gigantic bat, here again exactly matching the imagery of the choreography which Christopher Bruce described often to the dancers as the jagged flight of bats, the arch of their evil wings. To Nadine Baylis it also symbolized the enclosed world of the womb in which the fallen angels are forever bound; for them there is no redemption, no birth into the light. It is a cold, desolate place—the womb of time, containing them endlessly, living in its darkness.

In designing the set Nadine Baylis drew upon her own ideas of evil, and it seemed to her that the revelation about the concentration camp where human skin was made into lampshades was, as she describes it, "the most terrifying thing I have ever found out about human beings". This is hell, a world of total evil, in which those who owned those decorations from human flesh lived. This terrible memory darkened her imagination, giving to the set this sense of a kind of membrane that surrounded the dancers, hinting at this same obscenity. It was an image that also suggested the costume design, where the rags in which the dancers were dressed were, to the designer, "as if their skin had been pulled off them by hooks", containing this idea of torture and medieval terror.

The dancers are like beggars—hell's derelicts, begging at the gates of paradise. Nadine Baylis sees the image of beggars as a timeless one; it belongs to no century nor any people, and by this she wished to accentuate the idea that the fallen angels existed in a world beyond time and space, eternally ringed by their own solitude, the huge circular cavern of their oblivion.

As the dancers are dressed in rags with their fluttering wings, so there is also something blatant and sensual about them. The girls have one breast partly exposed beneath thin nylon, while John Read's lighting has turned their exposed flesh sometimes to the colour of putrefaction. This effect of bare skin, hung with wisps of tattered clothes, almost as if they had rotted away, gives to the dancers a quality of decaying sensuality that is so marvellously evoked in the dance. The flesh here and how it is lit—like dead skin, or marble or sometimes almost translucent—is as much a part of the costumes as are the rags or the loin-cloth in which the Christ-figure of Zoltan Imre is dressed.

As Nadine Baylis had planned, the *décor* leaves something more for the light, and John Read lit it in flickering flames from an inner hell. At the same time he was able to achieve a kind of spiritual radiance of blue light (accepted by mystics and clairvoyants as the light from the other world) during Lucy Burge's solo; or in other moments to turn the limbs to marble or graven stone.

The power and terrible beauty of the set and costumes exist in the same world as the choreography and the music, all drawn together within the light from hell. It is, one realized, the result of the closest collaboration between all those involved in the ballet, but more than that: it is the joining of separate images, felt by a group of artists, into a whole, a single vision.

5. The creation of "Black Angels"

It is said that when Bach began a new composition he dressed in his finest suit, with cravat and powdered wig, to mark the solemnity of the occasion. The creation of a ballet begins with no such formality—the dancers in a weird assortment of clothes, the choreographer in sagging green woollen tights with holes in them. Beyond the Ballet Rambert studio in Chiswick, one sees a panorama of rooftops and red chimneys; beneath, the traffic roars down the High Road.

There has been a class for the first hour and a half of the day, and, after a break for coffee, the dancers assemble in the studio where the choreographer is alone; having warmed up he improvises a few studies, watching in the long mirror at the end of one wall. There are to be six dancers—three men and three girls—Catherine Becque, Lucy Burge, Zoltan Imre, Bob Smith, Leigh Warren and Sylvia Yamada. These are to be the companions of my imagination over the next few weeks.

They complete their exercises, and then gather round the choreographer, while he explains to them the theme of the music as he will see it in his ballet. He has decided to take the pattern—Departure, Absence and Return—to symbolize the fall, the desolation and the Redemption of mankind, using the fallen angels of Christian theology as his protagonists. It is to be a work in which the eternal struggle between light and darkness is to end on a note of hope, the triumph of good over evil. At this stage the dancers do not listen to the music, but immediately begin work on the first section, "Night of the Electric Insects".

At once the choreographer crystallizes his ballet around three opening images. As the dancers run onto the stage, flung from heaven on the shuddering flight of the music, the first pose is a fall on the right shoulder, the legs hooked grotesquely in the air as if they clutched it for support; then they lurch upright in an image of terrible lamentation. They crawl forwards, as if swimming through the lake of fire, the heads then raised to gasp a breath of the cruel air. One couple cling to each other in their grief; a man stoops while the girl leans backwards across his body, then to be flung from him in a wide angled leap.

95

Much emphasis in these opening movements is given to the arms. "You must make them writhe like snakes," Bruce tells them; and again asks that the hands should be hooked like claws. There is, in this first section of the choreography, no sense of the once bright angels of God; these are debased beneath the human, so that they can only crawl on their bellies like maimed animals through the atrocious fire.

Each group of movements is demonstrated by the choreographer, taking the place of the male dancer in double work, while the dancer watches him. In one such pose he calls out to Lucy Burge, "Throw yourself on him as if you'd stick to him: it mustn't look like a formal *lift*." One upward extending movement with the arm raised he describes as being "like a cry of pain", while to give a portrait of enclosed movements, where the body is circled inwards, he tells the dancer it is "as if your inside is being torn out: it is like eating your own soul".

One sees how the ballet begins to grow organically from these first images, where the sad, swimming gesture is repeated when the dancers are upright, their arms groping before them as a blind man might feel the darkness, grasp in anguish the empty air. At times the dancers will wait while Christopher Bruce improvises alone certain images, then reshapes them, watching their patterns form in the mirror.

"That's good. I like that," a dancer calls out as he shapes a pose for Sylvia Yamada; then instructs her partner to turn her slowly in a double somersault. The atmosphere is relaxed, almost jokey; one begins to notice the different personalities as the ballet begins to form: there is one dancer who interpolates a series of wise-cracks, or sarcastic comments; a girl who seems over-intent, unsure, almost too anxious to please, whom Bruce treats with particular gentleness and patience, always encouraging her, seeking to reassure; one who works with a particular concentration, a little apart, less extrovert than the others. Yet, however relaxed the atmosphere, there is a profound seriousness in the work which makes these moments of relaxation and jokes essential.

Slowly the images begin to coalesce, sometimes taught to a dancer or her partner individually, then fitted into the total pattern; at others demonstrated to all the dancers together. There is no sense of a shared grief in them, but only of solitariness; and this is correct theologically since the state of the damned is one of isolation and eternal absence from God. This is why Christopher Bruce tells the dancers that their entry must not be entirely co-ordinated: "Each one of you", he tells the dancers, "is damned singly and alone."

Towards the end of this section of the music, the dancers huddle together; the heads are flung back in anguish, then the arms are raised piteously. Bruce tells them how they must catch here the sobbing of the music, how it sinks with them and how it raises them again, arms lifted to the indifferent skies. "You must", he says, "have weeping arms." In a tragic gesture a man cradles his arms as if holding a child. Then the three couples break apart in movements suggesting their lonely, brutal and loveless copulation.

This provides a little light relief from the Joker in this small band of dancers: "What's going on?" he calls out to the choreographer, to which he receives the amiable reply, "Just what you think." Another complains that it is a bit like "the last tango in Chiswick".

These three separate duets cause the greatest difficulty, so that the whole afternoon session is devoted to them. Catherine Becque crawls forwards on her stomach, the man's body arched above her; Lucy Burge is swung round by her partner, her legs clasped to his waist; Sylvia Yamada is held upside down, one foot hooked around her partner's neck. To each of these *pas de deux* Christopher Bruce adds an extension, where the dancers slide across one another, or push each other across the floor like the intertwined copulations of serpents.

The afternoon session ends when the dancers "walk through" the whole of the ballet as they have learned it so far. They have completed the first section, "Night of the Electric Insects". In working time it has taken from 11.30 a.m. until 1.50 p.m. and from 2.45 p.m. until 4 p.m.—a fraction over three and a half hours. In performance time it has covered less than two minutes.

2nd day

The atmosphere on the second day is different, since the first excitement of creating a new ballet has passed with its nervous relaxations into small jokes, the air of slight unease. One feels that the dancers have settled into a routine of work, now more sure of the music and the choreographic language.

The dancers run through the previous day's work, and Christopher Bruce carefully articulates one *enchaînement* for Zoltan Imre, dividing it into three grouped phrases. "Your arms", he tells Imre, "must hang down, as if you neither knew nor cared where they should fall. Then you leap upwards, as though you have been scorched by the flames." Imre listens intently with a deep inner concentration so marked in his dancing, which has a strange visionary quality, as if he heard the music in echo, listened to the calling of far voices. Bruce then works on a new *lift* with his partner, Sylvia Yamada. "She must come to you", the choreographer says, "as if for a moment you did not know she was there."

A pose from their copulation *pas de deux* is extended, so that Imre holds her with her legs hooked round his body, one arm hanging free like a broken wing. As she sinks backwards through his legs he staggers away from her, his hand still clutching her upraised foot. He looks dazed, even demented—head lolling, eyes sightless and mouth agape. "At this moment," Christopher Bruce tells him, "I want you almost insane, with an empty grin on your face." To Sylvia Yamada he says, "I want your body twisted, as if drawn on a rack." One feels that the intense emotional quality of these *pas de deux*, not fully drawn on the previous day, is now beginning to reach through to the dancers. They seem to feel in their limbs the flames of their damnation, sinking and rising again in the lake of fire. Graphically the choreographer tells them, "You are being burnt to a frazzle, like copulating crisps."

The *pas de deux* in the same section between Lucy Burge and Bob Smith is also reworked into an image of desolating beauty —the girl swung round him in broken arcs that look like a memory of her soaring days in the world of God; then her body falls in its spent flight, as his sags forward on the last descending phrase of the music.

After completing this superb picture, Bob Smith retires to take up his favourite position, sitting on the piano lid where, apparently, he can most comfortably relax. He is a free, independent spirit—of all the angels, the one most likely to rebel.

The choreographer then moves on to the second section of the music, "Sounds of Bones and Flutes". Again, as in the first section, he makes the opening statement in three connected images: the first, a loping run for all the dancers diagonally across the stage, with a little skip after the first five paces; this leads into a defiant, stamping dance which Bruce describes as the devils' dance, and this is followed by a grotesque little sequence like a drunken tap-dance.

It is extraordinary to see the range of emotion compressed into these three short sections. The first is like the running of whipped curs, broken and defeated; then there is this thrust of arrogance, the first assumption of diabolical pride, followed at once by the little jigging dance which is a kind of mockery of simple human joys, now beyond their reach or their understanding. Bruce urges the dancers in the second section to prance; they must, he says, be defiant even in their fall. He describes it as "a hideous drunken revel". It is indeed the insolent, military strut of the rebels against God.

In this scene, as in the earlier *pas de deux* of copulation, the choreographer links the two images of delight and anguish—a joy snatched savagely even as it crumbles into disgust. As Lionel Johnson writes in his poem, *The Dark Angel*:

> Apples of ashes, golden bright;
> Waters of bitterness, how sweet!
> O banquet of a foul delight,
> Prepared by thee, foul Paraclete!

Yet this defiance cannot be maintained. They run off balance across the stage, as if at any moment they would topple into the pit of hell. Then they recall the steps of their grimacing little skips, after which, in three wide leaps, they recover again the arrogance of their devils' dance. Here the choreography is very closely woven, as the initial statements return but set within a different context. Bruce tells them, "You are bewitched, possessed: you hardly know the movements you are making". This big, strutting dance shows how, for the first time, they have accepted their fate with a kind of hideous exultation. "You must let everything go," Bruce tells them, during the grotesque little tap-dance. "Your bodies must be loose like skeletons." And so they seem; one watches them jigging in the wind.

This section of the music closes in an extraordinary procession, the bodies clinging to one another, jolting along in a straggling line. They are like a group of refugees fleeing from the wrath of God. They are led by one man, who alone is not defeated; he struts and preens, an idolater of his own image. One dancer (Zoltan Imre) breaks free; he is left on the stage alone.

Here, to open the third section, comes the first solo—a dance for Imre of strange wistful beauty, sketched in frail and broken lines against the music. Piteously and tentatively he tries to raise his arms in the form of a cross; now he seems to be listening to the distant music of the angels in heaven. He is like one haunted, although whether by a memory or an intimation we cannot guess; but as he sinks to his knees he turns his face upwards in yearning to the empty skies.

> Oh, I'll leap up to my God! Who pulls me down?
> See, see, where Christ's blood streams in the firmament!

Here again the choreographer achieves the same compression of images that of other artists only the poet can attain. In fallen man we sense both the memory and the anticipation of his Redeemer, and we see the Redeemer himself first emerge into mortality, his arms, even as they stretch wide in the cradle (here superbly echoed by the choreographer in one image where the man crucified rocks as if still in his mother's arms) are also stretched outwards on the Cross.

That fine poet, R. S. Thomas, encompasses the same idea that is caught so beautifully here in the dance, when he writes:

101

Birth of a Ballet

And in the foreground
The tall Cross,
Sombre, untenanted,
Aches for the Body
That is back in the cradle
Of a maid's arms.

The day's work ends here, with only one dancer left, and a single image to haunt the mind.

3rd day

When the dancers assemble, Christopher Bruce makes further changes to the three *pas de deux* in the first section and to what he calls the "crazy march" that concludes it. The interlinked procession is dropped, though this is to be formed in a different design at the end of the march. In its place is substituted what he describes as "the devil's walk"—a high goose-step with the raised leg bent and the head thrown back in a kind of savage defiance. Slowly this begins to disintegrate, so that the dancers seem barely able to lift their limbs; finally they pause, crouched at the back of the stage. "You must be like bats," the choreographer says, "evil and clinging".

The earlier *pas de deux* are given further elaboration in detail. Catherine Becque and her partner, Leigh Warren, are coiled around one another in a grotesque coupling; yet within it, during certain poses when she rests her head against his encircling arm, there is still some tenderness. She and her partner look the youngest and most vulnerable of these six dancers, and one feels that a hint of true love, even its most distant echo, lingers in this last exhausted embrace. For Bob Smith and Lucy Burge, the movement where he swings her around his body with one of her arms hanging loose is now extended so that she releases the other arm and is held only by her legs gripping his waist in an attitude of total abandonment. "You must fly so low," the choreographer tells her, "that your hair brushes the stage." Sylvia Yamada is no longer held with one leg around her partner's neck; now, still upside down, she is

102

wheeled in big circles, her parted legs extended in the air like spokes of a wheel. Then she is hooked by her arms and legs to the front of his body, so that she seems to be sticking there, sucked obscenely against him.

The dancers writhe and roll over one another in a hideous tangle of arms and legs that are like the tentacles of sea creatures that rise from this lake of the damned. These are images, not of human love, but of the fierce mating of beast on beast, or even the copulations of insects grossly enlarged.

During the sections of lament, the "weeping arms" the choreographer demanded seem to rise now from the depths, an image of the psalmist's words:

> Out of the depths have I cried to you,
> O, Lord; Lord, hear my voice.

The arms circle inwards on their bent bodies, as though they tore out their own entrails.

Bruce tells the dancers at the end of their "crazy march" to pose "as if you were in silhouette, almost like a frieze". It is against this background that Zoltan Imre begins his solo which he had been taught the previous afternoon. This is an astonishing creation, lit by the music with a kind of shimmering light that is not of this world, on which he shapes, so hesitantly, the ghost of a prayer. It is dancing that whispers, a voice spoken inwardly, when he tries to tell the others of a vision he has seen, though not so much seen as come upon him like a visitation. As so often the poet expresses this most truly. Elizabeth Jennings writes:

> Prayer yet could be a dance
> But still a cross.

When he forms so tentatively the figure of a cross, he is standing almost off balance as though he stretched his whole body upwards to listen to the words of Redemption, to cling to them fading, even by his finger-tips. In a clash of discords he falls, the vision gone. It is as if he had been struck blind by unearthly light.

He is haunted, stunned by what he has seen and heard. The

choreographer says to him, "it is as if the shadow of the Cross had fallen across you".

The figure of the Devil (Bob Smith) approaches this huddled, kneeling man, poses arrogantly in a *half-plié* so that Imre rests his head on the other's leg. The Devil draws away and Imre falls, clutching at the other's ankles as he marches forward in his strutting walk. The *pas de deux* between the two men that follows is built in heavy, sculptural blocks, held together by an inner tension, so that the conflict between dark and light is joined but not resolved. "You are just a body that is being thrown around," the choreographer tells Imre. "It has to be both a spiritual and a physical conflict. As you fight with the Devil, you fight also with your own dark angel. The Devil is tearing your flesh apart."

At one moment in the *pas de deux* Imre pulls away so far from the other's clasped hand that they almost topple; then, against his will, he is forced to turn and see the Devil's face. "You are like a child at this moment," Bruce tells him. "You see evil for the first time out of your own innocence."

This majestic conflict, told in slow, tortured, at times almost acrobatic poses, achieves part of this sense of tension and spiritual conflict by a brilliant use of the two dancers' highly different styles—Bob Smith, earthy, with wide, arrogant flashes of his limbs like strokes of lightning cutting the darkness; Imre, far more lyrical, achieving the effect of a kind of blurred line, like thoughts barely caught, sketched with a trembling hand. The one dancer is elemental, to act as a perfect foil to the other's spirituality.

The Devil frees himself, springs into a savage, jagged turn *en attitude* like the leap of a flame caught in a gust of air. His solo is composed of wide, flamboyant movements, while his arms draw hieroglyphs around his body and face, as though he wrestled with a nest of snakes. It is a celebration of violence, of brute force—the triumph of physical evil over spiritual waverings and doubts. Yet it is no easy triumph, for these snake-like arms flail around his body, as if they struck at him with their fangs. Even at this stage, half-completed, it is a remarkable solo—brutal, yet quivering with an inward fear, a torment which

104

he cannot shake off with his arms. It is a picture of what Eliot describes as:

> The intolerable shirt of flame
> Which human power cannot remove.

The day ends with this solo not completed, for both the dancer and the choreographer are exhausted, not only from physical tiredness but from the endless struggle of all true choreography, to make the spirit articulate through the flesh.

4th day

It is difficult for the choreographer, Christopher Bruce tells me, to sustain the enthusiasm of the dancers over the whole period of creating a ballet, particularly working as he does directly on them without the details of the choreography set in his mind before he begins. He has to rely on the free movement of his imagination as it leads him from one phrase to the next. This demands intense powers of concentration in order to grasp each fleeting image as it rises from the unconscious. At the same time there are the different personalities of the dancers to be considered; each must be treated in a manner to which his or her personality will most easily respond. Some have to be coaxed, some to be bullied a little; others need continual encouragement, others again seem almost to resent it. This little group of six dancers is wonderfully responsive, yet there are bound to be frictions and tensions, both between each other and in relation to the choreographer.

He has to take them into his confidence to the extent that they must be able to follow his imagination, but not too far or else they may begin to make their own elaborations to his choreographic ideas. Some learn fast, others more slowly; each at first visualizes the images Bruce demonstrates to them in terms of their own physical build and temperament, responding in different ways according to their own inner creativity. They are not puppets or mimics, and he would not wish them to be so; they are creative artists in their own right.

It is fascinating to observe, in the pauses between each section of the dance as it is created, how they will improvise their own variation upon what they feel might be the next phrase composed for them by the choreographer, and these free improvisations—though he does not make use of them himself—are sketched by the dancers in strict accordance with the style of the movements they have already learned. They have, in fact, grasped intuitively the choreographic language of the work, its own particular nuances.

As the ballet develops one gains a closer understanding of the manner in which Christopher Bruce works. He appears to know in advance the opening phrase of a new section of the ballet; having taught this to the dancers, at first by them following him and then with him leading the dancing, the impetus of these phrases will carry him through to the next *enchaînement* by a kind of intuitive glimpse into its development.

The choreography is not a series of phrases, each joined to the next, rather a "carrying through" of the completed image into its harmonious extension; in much the same way the writer is carried through by the rhythmic impetus of his words, so that the next phrase grows almost of its own volition, and is often completed before he has grasped consciously what it has expressed. This is particularly true in poetry where the phrases rise in completed groups from the subconscious, rather than form themselves by any process of rational analysis; they will come entire, sometimes even in completed stanzas to which only minor alterations will be needed. Poetry, like choreography, the art to which it is most closely akin, sometimes just happens: the logic, the shaping and the craft come later. As Paul Valéry says of the poet, "he is both a cool scientist and a subtle dreamer". This indeed seems to me to compress the art of Christopher Bruce and all true choreographers into a single sentence.

Christopher Bruce puts this idea more simply to the dancers during a pause in the morning's work. "I see the most wonderful images five minutes before I go to sleep, but next day I've either forgotten them or else find they're impossible to express in movement." One realizes how the choreographer is forced, through the physical limitations of the body, to modify his own concepts; they are not quite what he imagined, nor could they ever be. I recall Natalia Makarova saying to me, "One seeks always for the spiritual content of the dance, but it's not easy to achieve with two legs!"

A further difficulty arises for Bruce in that he has a highly personal style. This means that the steps are reproduced with sometimes a different emphasis, thus placing him at one further remove from his own inner vision; one sees, but, as St Paul says, "in a glass darkly".

"Let's do some steps," Bruce tells the dancers.

After a moment's thought he demonstrates the first sequence —a long, padding run, sure-footed, through the empty spaces of the music. It is full of menace—the leopard's prowl, moving from the back of the stage directly to confront the audience. When the dancers have learned this, Bruce extends it into a spare, angular dance, shaped a little like the "skeleton dance" in the earlier section, but now defiant, as if an animal bared its fangs. It is remarkable how violent a shift of emotion can be obtained in two *enchaînements*, while, at the same time, each grows out of the other, not only in terms of design but also in emotional development. This dance and the section which follows are jaunty, even sardonic, like a twisted smile.

Now Bruce sharpens the images, sets the dancers flying in what he describes as a "diabolical carnival". He uses both *arabesques* and *jetés*—of all dance steps the most explicit in their sense of flight. At one moment he asks the dancers to hold a pose, making a tiny break in the flow of the dance, which is, in fact, more of a transition. "You must pause," he says, "but you must also keep on dancing, rest for a moment against the music." One sees exactly what he means; for the dancers are held there in their flight as gulls may be seen wheeling away against the wind.

The creation of this part of the ballet goes more freely than any so far; from each completed phrase when he dances it with the others Bruce is able to form the next pose or group of steps, the movements carrying him through to their extension. He has to work less on his own, trying out ideas to the mirror, as a

writer might search his imagination for the exact word to complete his thought; now it flows more easily, reaching beyond the created dance to catch these hidden images as they emerge. One recalls the magnificent description of the poet by Dryden as one who "moves the sleeping images of things to the light".

The Company's musical director, Adam Gatehouse, who is watching the rehearsal and following the music from the score, points out a discrepancy between the musical count and that of the dance. Bruce decides that at certain phrases the dancers will move through the music rather than follow its beat exactly. His use of music is very flexible: at times the steps will grow out of the musical phrase, matching it exactly; at others the music is, as it were, fitted round the dance, so that now and again there are more dance images than musical space in which to contain them. This occurs almost at the end of the present section where two very powerful statements—a twisted, mocking image of the Cross made with the dancers' arms and then a fall onto the knees in a contemptuous gesture of prayer—extend fractionally the space available for them in the music, so that some compression of the choreography is demanded.

The dancers are not to continue after the lunch break, so that the day's work closes when they have run through the whole of the second and third section of the music completely. Christopher Bruce then thanks them, and they are equally happy. It has been a good day, one that comes all too rarely for any artist, yet when it comes—to writer or dancer alike—it comes almost like a benediction.

5th day

One of the dancers, Bob Smith, is away ill, while Sylvia Yamada has an injured foot so that she can only walk through the choreography, but Christopher Bruce is able to continue with his beleaguered band of angels. Further details are added, rather in the way a painter might highlight sections of his canvas, darkening the shadows, or altering the manner in which the light falls.

As the dancers wait to begin their first loping run at the beginning of the earlier section, Bruce instructs them to intertwine their arms and limbs: "crawl over one another like serpents," he says. "You are like a nest of snakes." They must look almost a single creature—"like a Hydra", he tells them.

When this part has been completed, Bruce moves on to the "Danse Macabre" which is section five of the music. There are still some problems in reconciling the dance count with the musical beat which is set in "sevens"—the magical symbol to which Crumb continually reverts. Near the end of this dance the moment when they shape a cross with their arms is violently compressed, so that, Bruce tells them, "it must appear hugely speeded up, like images that flicker in a nightmare". He instructs the dancers in the sinister, padding run which opens the section to raise their arms slowly as they advance towards the audience, so that by the end they are curved like jagged wings. The choreographer uses the arms with great subtlety, so that they speak in many different accents—as wings, as serpents, as the uncoiling of fearful tentacles. A particularly striking image is when one arm is allowed to fall loose, like a broken wing, symbol of their lost paradise. As Matthew Arnold writes:

> Then not the nectarous poppy lovers use,
> Nor daily labour's dull, Lethaean spring,
> Oblivion in lost angels can infuse
> Of the soiled glory, the trailing wing.

In a later section of the "Danse Macabre", he sharpens the accents into a kind of jerky strut, asking the dancers to imagine that they are moving in the flicker of strobe lighting. Now he incorporates gestures denoting fiendish laughter and the vile cramming of food into their mouths as if they were eating human flesh. These images, he tells the dancers, are a recurrent symbol in the paintings of Hieronymus Bosch.

The fifth section of the music ends with the sound of voices counting from one to the magical seven in Hungarian, and leaves the dancers drifting towards the front of the stage, hovering there on outspread wings; it has the evil quiet of hawks motionless in the air above their prey.

The creation of Black Angels

The sixth section—opening the second part of the work—is based on the *andante* of Schubert's *Death and the Maiden* quartet, here played to the sound as of a concert of viols; the composer instructs that it must sound "like the fragile echo of ancient music".

Christopher Bruce begins work on a *pas de deux* between the "Christ-Figure" (Zoltan Imre) and Catherine Becque, the most angelic looking of the dancers. He carries her on his back in the shape of a cross, then falls under her weight. This reminds one of Eric Gill's beautiful Stations of the Cross in Westminster Cathedral, where, at one of the early Stations, Christ is seen falling beneath the Cross as he carries it to Calvary.

Behind him the other dancers form a mocking procession; they squat down, crouching like toads. Then by a most beautiful transposition the next pose is of Catherine Becque held in parallel above Imre, hovering there like a watchful angel. As Hamlet says, as if to invoke the same pose:

> Save me, and hover o'er me with your wings,
> You heavenly guards.

A whine of icy wind in the music draws the dancers away to the rear of the stage, blown backwards it seems into their dark caverns of air. The poses in the *pas de deux* reform, so that the girl is balanced across the male dancer in an image of soaring flight. The pose has something of the delicate beauty of the early Renaissance paintings where the angels come to minister to Christ, poised on the shimmer of their golden wings. Yet there is a deeper symbolism than this (for the ballet is full of hidden resonances, different layers of meaning) since it is also a picture of the angels of God speaking to men, as they do in the New Testament, within their mortal dreams. As Henry Vaughan, that great poet and mystic, writes:

> And yet, as angels in some brighter dreams
> Call to the soul when man doth sleep.

On this beautiful image the morning's work ends.

111

6th day

The designer for *Black Angels*, Nadine Baylis, brings in the first idea for a costume for Leigh Warren. It is made from strips of nylon, dyed black, and falls in two jagged wings, attached to the forearm just above the elbows. This is referred to by the dancers as the first prototype and is much admired. Leigh Warren turns a few swift *pirouettes*, observing himself in the mirror, to see how the wings look in movement.

At the beginning of this session, Christopher Bruce goes back over details of earlier work, indicating exactly how the hand should be held in one movement, so that it looks sharp and angular like the tip of a wing. He instructs the dancers to end the "Danse Macabre" with gestures indicating hysterical laughter that must be fitted into the gaps of their fragmented dance. In the section learned the previous day, when Zoltan Imre carries the tiny Catherine Becque across his back in the form of a cross, the dancers are instructed, when they follow this in procession, to indicate with their hands across the face the flow of falling tears.

The choreographer fills in the background for the remainder of the dancers while this *pas de deux* is in progress. One notices how the ballet is built around the two symbols of wings and the Cross; how the one, by a series of transformations, will reform as the other, so that the central conflict of the ballet is symbolically maintained.

Two other dancers from the Company come into the studio to begin to learn the roles as understudies and second cast. While Bruce is instructing Imre in certain details, the dancers show their colleagues individually what they have learned. One feels a little sorry for the newcomers who have to pick up choreography, mounted on others, in bits and pieces when the time can be spared for them. They look somewhat isolated, a little disconsolate in the background, like guests who have not been invited to the party.

A constant figure in the studio is the choreologist, in this case a student choreologist, Marika Rennerfelt, who takes down every movement as it is created in Benesh movement notation, so that finally a complete record of the ballet is made for the Company records. This will indicate even the smallest gesture, written in symbols on a type of musical stave, so that the ballet can be remounted on any future date, even if the choreographer and the dancers have forgotten certain details. It is a recent development; before this, choreographers had to rely solely on memory and on the memories of their dancers, so that an old classic work, like *Giselle*, for example, was passed down the years as the tradition was handed over from one generation of dancers to another.

The conductor also watches as many rehearsals of a new ballet as possible, following it from the score, so that he can catch any discrepancies between the music and the danced rhythms, and make any alterations to tempo that may be necessary. The designer will also observe the ballet as it progresses, in order to make sure her designs suit the quality of movement and do not impede the dancers or affect their "line".

By far the greatest part of this afternoon's rehearsal is given up to a big solo for Leigh Warren. While he is learning this the other dancers relax in their rest-room downstairs where they gossip, read and eat food from tins, on which dancers seem to thrive. If they are to take no part in one section of the ballet, they do not normally watch, preferring to see the completed version when they are next required in the studio.

Leigh Warren and the choreographer work very swiftly on the solo, one movement growing out of another with a wonderful fluidity. He is very quick to learn, catching the quality of the images as if at first glance, and reproducing them with a fine accuracy. This allows Bruce to keep his own creative rhythm moving, so that there are few moments when he has to pause for long consideration, or form and discard variations of different poses until he discovers one that satisfies him; instead, he adds new phrases with great fluency to those he has already created, and he and Warren work in perfect accord. The solo, which takes over two hours to compose, lasts one and a half minutes, but it is a superb dance, built on long open lines of rare beauty.

113

"It's a long dance," Bruce tells him, to which the dancer gaspingly replies, "I think it's the longest dance in the world." One notices how Leigh Warren has some difficulties with certain movements only because he has not (as he puts it) yet "begun to feel them properly". Dancing is indeed far more a matter of sensation than one had imagined; it is not sufficient just to copy the movement invented by the choreographer, but one must feel it as well, both physically and emotionally. Occasionally the dancer will say, "Can you give me another step?" in order to cope with difficult linking passages. Certain points are explained to him by means of expressive metaphors: for example, at one point Bruce tells him, "it is as if you are breaking out of a chrysalis"; at another, that his movements must be "like those of a crouching ape", or "the twitching of some huge insect". Sometimes the choreographer will catch a glimpse of an extension to a movement within a single phrase of the dance when he will ask Leigh Warren to perform it again, so that he can recover it, almost like the recall of a memory.

The solo grows organically. With its sense of swooping flight the dancer looks as if he moves on the eddying currents of the air. To break these long, free lines Bruce introduces violent leaps from a crouching position, so that one senses an enclosed hatred erupting suddenly upwards like a spurt of flame.

When the other dancers return, Bruce links them to Leigh Warren's solo where they follow him as he crosses the stage in diagonal in a series of leaps. He adds an extension to their dance to conclude the day's work, so that, in its incomplete state, they may have something to start from the following morning. It has been a rewarding day, in which the central structure of the ballet is now firmly in place in a related pattern of *soli* and *pas de deux*. Like all works of art it grows through its own inner logic, rather than one imposed on it coldly from without; for there is this logic in creative art, which Keats described as "the truths of the imagination", that dispels all conflict between content and form.

The creation of Black Angels

The small cohort of angels is back to full strength with the return of the absent Satan (Bob Smith) who has a bad cold which he describes, with great fidelity to his role, as "an infernal nuisance". Christopher Bruce makes some amendments to Leigh Warren's solo. In order to give additional emphasis to one step, Bruce tells him, "At this point it's as if you spat in his face" indicating the prostrate "Christ-Figure" of Zoltan Imre. He then works with the other dancers by extending the phrase they had left incomplete the previous night. A further prototype costume arrives, a dress for Lucy Burge, at the moment far too wide at the waist.

As the dancers rework some of the earlier group and solo pieces one has an opportunity to study their different styles, and to see how cunningly these have been used by the choreographer. The youngest of the angels, Catherine Becque, has a lovely clear-cut line, matching her vivid personality; especially in flight, she swoops in the air like the curve of a swallow's wing. Lucy Burge, beautiful with her fine-drawn features and auburn hair, has a richer, more sensual way of movement; between these two one sees in miniature the continual difference between the dancer of the air and the dancer of the earth of whom the immortal exemplars are Taglioni and Elssler. Of the three girls, perhaps Sylvia Yamada has the most fluid style, the long flow of the dance like a ripple of water.

Of the men, Leigh Warren has great speed, stamina and a fine open line. Before rehearsals he likes to warm up in the studio wearing *point* shoes, taking up poses on *point* in order to strengthen his feet. Bob Smith is strong, extrovert, with a kind of flashing brilliance, the steps formed with a fierce intensity, perfectly suited to his role. As a contrast to this is the sensitivity, delicacy of feeling and a curious hesitancy in emotional expression of Zoltan Imre's dancing. For so large a man, he manages to achieve remarkable, almost fading movements, very gentle like a spent sigh. The contrast between the two men— one so strong and so physical in his approach to the dance, the

115

other so lyrical and seemingly so unsure—gives the ballet a remarkable sense of tension at its heart. This is not just in the different quality of movement they have been given for their duets, but the tension between two such contrasted personalities that seems to exist within their dancing.

At the end of the short morning's work, the dancers run through the whole ballet up to the point they have reached. This is the first time they have danced the opening section for a week, yet they remember it, even if, here and there, it is blurred in detail. Before they dance, they mark it out, just sketching the briefest abbreviation of each step while they think through the whole section. It is a fascinating recollection of visual memory.

Christopher Bruce further extends the duet between Bob Smith and Zoltan Imre, where the struggle between good and evil is intensified. In one mocking gesture Imre's arms are dragged out in the form of a cross: there is a sense of brutal triumph in the Devil's solo, created earlier and now dividing the two parts of the duet.

After lunch all the dancers assemble, and Christopher Bruce tells them briskly, "Right—now back to the bats." This is a working of the section following Leigh Warren's solo where the dancers crowd round him as he lies on the ground, as if about to tear him to pieces. This horrifying scene was created the previous day but then discarded; now it fits exactly into place, a moment of gloating viciousness. "Here", Bruce tells the dancers, "the music seems to lunge at him lying there. You must crowd round, as if seeking to devour him." He breaks away from them, for they are like harpies, stabbing at him with their claws, tearing the flesh. At one point Bruce corrects them saying, "I don't want all this dancing in time—not for bats!"

While the dancers relax, Bruce asks them to listen to the next section of the music. They lie on the floor in those attitudes of casual grace that belong only to dancers in repose. Bruce then works on a duet between Leigh Warren and Blake Brown, who has come in to understudy for Zoltan Imre in the afternoon. This is built as an *adagio* on very slow, flowing lines so that one pose seems to be absorbed by another; it has not the hard, unyielding quality of the previous *pas de deux* between Bob

Smith and Imre. At one point the dancers move, one close behind the other, in a beautiful mirror image that has a strange, undulating effect as if it were seen reflected in moving water. It seems the tides of all human misery carry them through each slow unfolding of their limbs. Earlier, in music of an unearthly weariness, the image of Christ carrying his Cross is again expressed by the two dancers, but here the Cross is not the fragile Catherine Becque, but the heavy body of a man, almost too great a burden to lift, too heavy, the music seems to say, for any man to bear.

Now the ballet is about to enter the exquisite singing passage of "God-Music", as the composer calls it. It is at this point in the work, as the choreographer sees it, that mankind becomes aware of the possibility of its Redemption; indeed all that has gone before awaited this moment, this sudden flooding of light against the darkness. It is, Christopher Bruce tells me, the section of the music that moves him most deeply, and it is here, one suspects, that he will achieve the finest part of his choreography.

The dancers go out of the studio, where the choreographer is left alone to listen to this music.

8th/9th day

Work on these two days was disrupted by the visit of a B.B.C. crew to make recordings of the Company to mark their fiftieth anniversary in June, 1976. However, Christopher Bruce was able to complete the duet between Zoltan Imre and Leigh Warren; also to compose a large section of an important solo for Lucy Burge to open the final part of the music—"The Return".

The duet for Imre and Warren develops into a profoundly moving vision of the Crucifixion, told in slow, unfolding poses between the two dancers, as though Christ were embraced by the Cross, held almost gently against its extended arms. One is reminded of the ancient Sequence in the liturgy for Good Friday, with its refrain:

117

Birth of a Ballet

Dulce lignum, dulces clavos,
Dulce pondus sustinet.[1]

Zimre rests against Leigh Warren's arms, almost as if he lay
against the beloved; here indeed the Cross "aches for the body"
as R. S. Thomas says in the poem quoted earlier. This whole
section is composed with perfect taste and judgement, with no
hint of realism, no over-statement or vulgar piety. This strange
encounter between the Redeemer and his Cross, evoked with
such tenderness in the choreography, here restates a later section
of the Sequence:

> Bend, proud tree, thy spreading branches,
>   Loosen thy rigidity,
> All that ruggedness begotten
>   Of thy stern heredity:
> Thine to throne the King of heaven;
>   Hold his body tenderly.

A small solo for Imre follows, drifting on the music as if on
expiring breath. Then he is laid across Lucy Burge in the attitude
of a Pietà, while the dancers gather round them in images of an
almost antique despair. Then they draw away, lean backwards
as if bedazzled: it is the moment, one feels, when the veil of the
temple was ripped apart, the graves opened, the dead, new risen,
walked the empty streets of Jerusalem. These are not the black
angels; they stand now for all mankind, caught in the sudden
brightness of a new day. It is a moment of great spiritual
beauty, recalling lines from a Nativity poem by John Heath-
Stubbs:

> The sacrifice, which is not made for them,
> The angels comprehend, and bend to earth
> Their worshipping way.

The solo that follows for Lucy Burge, as the figure of the
bereaved Mary, alternates between the long, flowing lines of a
serene acceptance of her grief and sudden violent movements
that are like anguished stabs of memory. The hands are shaped
in the form of prayers; tiny, stuttering steps are like small sobs

[1] Sweet the nails, and sweet the timber;
Sweet the load they bear aloft.

118

heard beneath the music. As if burdened by grief she falls to the ground, her cheek brushing the earth; then she rises with her arms and body open to the empty sky. One seems to watch the music reflected in the dancer's serenely beautiful face, so like that of a madonna of high Renaissance art, almost luminous in its response.

In this solo are contained images of birth; then, with one hand open against her cheek, she seems to be listening to the voice of the angel of the Annunciation, that most beautiful of all our world's encounters, so exquisitely evoked by Edwin Muir:

> Yet the increasing rapture brings
> So great a wonder that it makes
> Each feather tremble on his wings.

Again, in another gesture, she rocks a baby in her arms, and a hint of a smile touches her lips, recalling those days.

Amid the terrible grieving of this dance is also a sense that, when Christ lay in the tomb, Mary had taken over all the griefs and evils of the world which had been his burden and from which mankind would at the appointed hour be finally redeemed. Such an idea seems implicit in this dance, one of such terrible lamentation.

It is the nature of the dance to reveal spiritual truth without sentimentality, yet this is a very difficult thing to achieve. Here it brings a sense of wonder, the stillness of a vision attained. I do not think one can ask any more of the dance than that.

10th day

A considerable part of this afternoon's work is devoted to clarifying details of the choreography already completed, as well as adding to Lucy Burge's solo and the groupings of the dancers who are to frame it. At first the choreographer makes small additions to the duet between Zoltan Imre and Leigh Warren, in order to attain the greatest possible fluidity of movement, so that one has the sense that the Cross gathers the Body into its arms.

While Bruce works over this with the dancers, the others practice earlier sections of the ballet alone, so that one is seeing, in different parts of the studio, several isolated figures lost in their own deliberations, rather in the manner one might hear an orchestra tuning up before a concert, fragments of melody for a moment caught, then broken off again.

Bruce pays particular attention to the correct setting of the Pietà group; also where Imre stands, outspread above the dancers, then falls into their arms. Here the three girls hold him, as the woman held the dead body of Christ, and from this group Lucy Burge appears to begin her magnificent solo. She completes this, and the dancers, who have not seen it before, all applaud.

The choreographer then reverts to the second devils' dance from the earlier section, one that has caused him some difficulty in achieving the right shifts of emphasis among the dancers. They are shown more details in the use of the hands and arms, also particular attention is given to certain poses which, although almost unnoticeable in the flow of the dance, give to it a sense of arrested flight, like birds caught suddenly in a current of air. Christopher Bruce is now most concerned with matters of stress and dynamics, where there are often abrupt shifts within a single dance, that must be caught exactly in the manner the dancers phrase the steps. It is a question of detail, of shading a movement with the same care as a painter alters the falling of a shadow, or tips the canvas with a tiny fleck of light.

Far greater attention is now paid to the floor spacing of the group dances, and the whole pattern of the choreography is brought more closely together. There are still uncomfortable joins between sections that are now ironed out as the groups reform.

The dancers are dismissed early, so that Bruce can work further with Lucy Burge on her solo. A difficult moment, when she is brought to the ground by the weight of her griefs, is rehearsed several times, while meticulous attention is given to the placing of the hands and arms in one turn *en attitude*. One section is to be danced (Bruce tells her) "like the sound of broken sobs". Again he tells her, in the passage where she

121

seems to rock a baby in her arms, that "this is her memory of the Nativity", and the gesture is made without great clarity, but with a soft outstretching of the arms, blurred even, like the glimpse of a distant memory.

Here the choreography achieves the simplicity and the beautiful compression of images that one finds in lyric poetry written nearly a thousand years ago; to me it recalled those beautiful lines written by an anonymous poet in the eleventh century:

> Now goeth sun under wood—
> Me rueth, Mary, thy faire rode.
> Now goeth sun under tree;
> Me rueth, Mary, thy son and thee.[2]

Lucy Burge works for a long period with the choreographer until they are both exhausted; then it becomes difficult to achieve the right clarity for each step. This solo, seen now in its entirety, has become the great supporting arch of the whole ballet; it takes up all the music in section ten in one single span of movement—a dance as carefully structured and proportioned as the nave of a cathedral. The choreographer has lavished more detailed attention upon it than on any other section of the ballet, to achieve absolute clarity in its images. Lit by the unearthly light of the music, it is now as distant as an apparition glimpsed on the frontiers of eternity.

11th day

When the dancers arrive, Christopher Bruce resumes work on the devils' dance which still has not achieved quite the right amount of stress or the shifting of dynamics between each phrase. He is particularly concerned with those moments when the music seems suddenly to freeze, as if the blood congealed in the veins; then the dance must leap from the pose, suddenly naked, like the slash of a knife. Bruce adds details in the articulation of the arms to clarify the outline of this dance, its

[2] *Me rueth*: I grieve for; *rode*: face.

122

sense of frenzied movement. The dancers then run through the whole ballet until the end of Lucy Burge's solo.

As a result, there are more details to be improved: in Bob Smith's solo he is told to make the inward movement of his arms appear "as if you are eating in on yourself". A *lift* for Sylvia Yamada is reconstructed, but it is later on abandoned by the choreographer as being "too formal, too dancey". Further details are again added to Lucy Burge's solo. A beautiful gesture is included where both arms are raised upwards like a voice calling to the skies.

Christopher Bruce then works on section 11 of the music that follows Lucy Burge's solo. This he choreographs as a duet for the two other girls—Sylvia Yamada and Catherine Becque. He works slightly differently with them—first sketching out the dances at great speed and in broad outline, then returning to them in order, as he puts it, "to add the embellishments". This, one feels, is right, for it is a far more decorative dance than any he has yet composed in the ballet, created with a lavishness of detail, particularly in the placing of the hands and arms. It is, he says, "a dance of celebration, the arms flung upwards like joyful cries". Indeed it is extremely elaborate, thus in complete contrast to the pure lines of Lucy Burge's solo which preceded it.

One of the first embellishments he adds is to the hands. Here the prayers they speak are like the flutter of captive doves held in their arms. It is a design of beautiful delicacy, the hands upraised, quivering in the air. The ballet teacher of the Company, Gary Sherwood, remarks to me that they are more like cherubs now than fallen angels, and indeed there is truth in this: these two small, finely-built girls, are interlinked by their hands like the dancing choirs of angels one sees above so many paintings of the Italian Renaissance. It is child-like, with a touching innocence; at one moment their dances, which are carefully counterpointed, carry gestures like those of children with skipping ropes.

When they link hands in a tiny procession, the picture is so elegant and intricate in its line that one is reminded of the jewelled figures some great silversmith like Cellini might use.

123

They have together the trust of children, the same innocence. But it is not a mortal joy; it is one that is indeed angelic. It brings to mind the remark of Basilius, who was bishop of Caesarea in the fourth century, when he writes: "We remember those who now, together with the angels, dance the dance of the angels around God."

These are the angels of whom Edmund Spenser wrote:

> How oft do they their silver bowers leave,
> To come to succour us that succour want!
> How oft do they with golden pinions cleave
> The flitting skies, like flying Pursivant.

This duet brings a kind of delicacy, a sense of unwordly beauty, that is new to the ballet. After the eruptions of hatred in the early scenes, the spirits of the damned struggling through their rivers of fire, these dancers are of the air, so bright, so sure-footed, as if they balanced on the winds.

The dance then grows more gentle; now, the choreographer tells them, "you must soften the movements as the music softens to its close". In some ways this little duet brings back the sense of innocence that was so much a part of Bruce's earlier ballet, *Ancient Voices of Children*; it has all the wisdom, all the enchantment of the angels of God.

12th day

Christopher Bruce now completes the little skipping dance for the two bright angels, closing it on a pose where they are balanced on *half-point* as though hovering in the air. This exactly matches the long, quivering note on the violins, magically extended, which is like the distant rustle of their wings. The Christ-Figure of Zoltan Imre, who lies with Lucy Burge prostrate across his body, now rises; slowly he advances, she with her head on his shoulder. The angels fall, dazzled and afraid. Bob Smith (Satan) creeps towards him on a slow, crooked walk, contorted with hatred, while his companion devil (Leigh Warren) advances from the other side. Then Satan leaps, uncoiling his body in a savage *jeté*, and Imre forces him aside in a gesture which Bruce describes as "how he would thrust a nightmare away".

This is the last, most desperate assault of the fallen angels against God, heard in the scream of their voices that now returns in the music. To quote John Heath-Stubbs again, so marvellously apposite to this moment in the ballet:

> Those with black shining feathers that scream and tear;
> The angels rending their bright hair
> Amid the fog and babel of crying voices . . .

Bruce tells both dancers that these leaps "must be like screams of pain; for Satan, it is as if he can contain his hatred no more". They fall: the victory over evil has been won.

It is a moment of extraordinary tenderness when the Christ-Figure gathers up these two evil spirits into his embrace, his hands behind their heads in a gesture almost of benediction. They move in procession towards the back of the stage, each separate angel drawn to him in the same way. Flanked by his two attendant angels, Imre raises himself above them with each hand on their shoulders.

The ballet is near its close now, but Bruce prefers to leave the final scene until later. Instead he reverts to filling in a background to the moment when Christ is seen carrying his Cross. Satan leaves him, and falls on one of the angels in a fierce, writhing copulation, a hideous echo of the first scene in the ballet, now placed in brutal counterpoint against the sad journey of the Redeemer.

Many additional background movements will have to wait, the choreographer says, until the set has been designed; then he will be able to see them in their correct perspective. He describes very eloquently how "there will be, standing round the edges of the stage, these desolate lonely figures, as if lost on the empty moon".

In this last section of the ballet one notices how a work packed with movement is drawn so quietly to its close. It is gentle and serene, matching the soft tremors of the music that seem to lighten a desolate landscape on which the battle has been joined and finally won. Now the dancers are drawn around the figure of Christ to music that is like an exhausted sigh.

The atmosphere at the rehearsal has been more light-hearted than at any time since the first day. The dancers know that they have almost completed the ballet: they are like children on the last day of term. When they run through the completed work, including additional rehearsals of the two devils' dances that have caused so many problems, they dance in a mood that is almost one of jubilation, rejoicing over their work, freely and with daring, knowing in their hearts that what has been done over the past three weeks has been finely done.

13th day

The morning's work begins with some further additions and alterations to the pose where Zoltan Imre rises above the dancers, supporting himself on the shoulders of the other men. Now Christopher Bruce arranges that he shall fall backwards into the arms of the girls standing behind the men. This pose has an extraordinary architectural beauty that brings cries of approval from the dancers. Bruce also makes some additions to the movements of the devils in this scene, where they are to form a series of constricted and tortured poses, as if (Bruce tells them) "they flinched beneath the lash of a whip"— presumably that of their own anguished consciences.

Nearly all the rest of the time is taken up with a new solo for Zoltan Imre in which is expressed the theme of redemption, towards which the choreography has been moving. Bruce tells him that "joy must burst out of your body"—a brilliant description of the dance which grows from inward to outward gestures, in direct contrast to the earlier devils' dances where so many phrases constrict and turn in on the body. The arms open skywards as the petals of a flower might turn to the sun. It is joy growing from the heart. "You must let your limbs float on the music," the choreographer says.

The solo opens with gestures that echo those Imre made when earlier he heard for the first time the voice of his redemption, and tried in vain to express what he had heard, speaking with his opened arms. But then the pose was only half formed; it seemed to hesitate, in the same manner as one will reach for words and know these words are not sufficient. Now his arms open wide, confident and assured: there is no ambiguity in the message now. They are now exultant, as the body is, turned upwards towards a sky winged with angels. The mood of this dance recalls the sublime canticle of Zachary, recorded by St Luke:

> For in the tender compassion of our God
> the morning sun of heaven will rise upon us,
> To shine on those who live in darkness
> under the cloud of death.

This solo is constructed with great subtlety in dynamics, where the movements are differently paced even within one short *enchaînement*. At times they will be softened; at others they will flash like reflected light. These rapid changes of pace seem to indicate the sudden flooding of emotion that comes to us and is known by the irregular beating of the heart. Sometimes the arms cut the air like the sweep of wings; at others they rest upon it, floating, cloud-like, across the surface of the music. The dance incorporates tiny, stuttering movements of the feet that are like snatches of excited breath, the flutter of the heart.

Christopher Bruce and Zoltan Imre work at great speed, going back over certain passages, cutting here or changing a gesture there, until the design is complete. Always there is this sense of urgency in the dance, the coming of a swift delight; yet its ceaseless ebb and flow indicates also those periods of tranquillity when joy is recalled in a moment's pause to wonder and to praise.

The dancers are then recalled, and the whole ballet up to the end of Zoltan Imre's solo is performed, now with a kind of thrust and daring one had not seen before, the three great solos set in place like jewels.

Christopher Bruce tells the dancers that the final section of the ballet will treat Zoltan Imre's solo fugally—first with one dancer, then with two duets. When they leave the studio he remains to listen to the music, as if to greet, in the secrecy of his imagination, those who dance for himself alone.

14th day

The choreography for *Black Angels* is completed in the late afternoon in an atmosphere as casual and relaxed as when Christopher Bruce began the ballet. He thanks the dancers with obvious sincerity for the work they have achieved over the past three weeks, and they respond with a reticence so typical of dancers and one or two nice jokes. Then they go home for the weekend.

The creation of a work of art ends so, in whatever medium— some fatigue, a certain relief, but, most of all, a feeling of loss and a tiny ache of disappointment, lingering but impossible to localize. I have known it so often, writing the last sentence of a book, and it cannot be different for a choreographer who writes his words with human bodies in the strange intimacies of his art.

Christopher Bruce began the day by making some alterations to Zoltan Imre's solo upon which the fugal construction of the last section of the music is to be based. The emotional pattern of this solo and the dances that are to follow begin to clarify. At first his arm movements are restricted, then they open, and only towards the end of the solo do they close again. The black angels had begun to hope for their redemption, as one could see in the dances of the previous day, but slowly, in terrible understanding, they realize that this hope is unavailing. Redemption is not for them; they are to be excluded for ever when once they believed they could be saved.

This idea emerges in choreography of the utmost subtlety and daring as Lucy Burge, then Sylvia Yamada and Catherine Becque, and, finally, the two men join this dance in the same manner as different voices join a fugue. It is composed partly of steps they have performed earlier in the ballet, sometimes modified in detail, and partly shared fragments of each other's dance. We see again the little skipping steps from the duet for the two girls, the anguished invocations in Lucy Burge's arms, and, most frightening of all, the high goose-stepping march of Satan and his companion. Here also return the early cringing poses, broken in harsh, distorted lines, jagged like a flash of lightning.

Most poignantly of all, in his final solo Zoltan Imre recalls the voice of God that spoke to him out of his dream, so that he shapes once more, with the old hesitancy, the arms of the Cross. At one moment he turns his head aside, shielding his eyes from the light, recalling the great invocation of the Easter liturgy, "Lumen Christi" to which now he will never be able to respond.

The dance is formed in a circle moving round the stage in that endless ring of time by which the early philosophers sought to describe the world of eternity. Zoltan Imre's arms no longer open in a prayer, but like a cluster of thorns grow harshly against his body. The fallen angels recall, as if from a forgotten dream, the story of the Redemption, knowing with a terrible finality that it is one in which they will never share. They have, in a sense, been actors in a drama not for them, whose joyous conclusion it is for others to know; they can only grasp with their crooked hands the shadow of memory, the fading dream of a gallows on a hill.

The choreographer explains this to the dancers: "You are lonely, lost figures in a vast landscape, always now to be alone." In the fugue they each dance their own isolation; they are as alone as when the ballet began and the angels fell from heaven on the shuddering flight of music which now in echo returns.

The dancers freeze into their final poses, apart from one another, lost in their eternal solitude. Bob Smith as Satan advances towards the audience, his walk heavy with menace. If the ballet ends on a note of interrogation, it is also one of warning. Evil is real and ever present. It hovers over us; it is there always, Satan indeed, spread wide on his bat-like wings.

Maybe for them there is still a glimmer of hope, and when there is that, perhaps damnation is not eternal. For this is the terrible irony of the last section of the ballet: they begin to hope, to rejoice even, and now they find this joy is not and can never be their own. Here the choreographer wonderfully

129

captures the ambiguities in the closing page of the music. The last seven single notes are like questions asked, without any real hope of an answer, blindly to the unheeding skies. As the dancers freeze in their final isolation these notes also sound like the last stars one by one burning out, to leave only the night and a vast darkness.

6. The Ballet completed

"I had a vision of a face, an experience."

The ballet completed, with only the rehearsals to come, Christopher Bruce talked for the first time about the work. It was detached from him now, even, as he said "something mysterious" whose genesis he did not find it easy to recall. But he remembered this first glimpse—the face, the experience—that he had seen inwardly when he listened to the music, and from this the seed of the ballet was planted in his mind.

There are few experiences for an artist more mysterious than this first glimmer of a work as it comes to him; not a flash, not a sudden inspiration, less palpable than that—a hint of the coming dawn when the horizon is lit from the hidden sun, a faint lessening of the darkness. The poets have described it many times, but in some perplexity, seeking the words. For example, the great French poet, Gérard de Nerval, writes: "I saw vaguely drifting into form, plastic images of antiquity, which outlined themselves, became definite and seemed to represent symbols of which I only seized the idea with difficulty."

For Christopher Bruce the ballet was found in its entirety in the music. "It gave everything to me, every movement arose out of it, the form and design were conditioned by it." He first discovered the music at the same time as Crumb's *Ancient Voices of Children*, but he decided he was not yet ready for *Black Angels*, so that he chose to work on the other score first. This he saw in terms of great spaces around the dancers, something childlike, with a sense of random movement. "I realized I could make steps to *Black Angels* in a way I could not for *Ancient Voices of Children* where they would look too contrived."

As he brooded over the music for many months before he began to compose, Bruce began to see isolated images, sometimes no more than single steps, and a glimpse of a total design that would incorporate a Christ-like figure and a Madonna. His intention was to use the figures of Christian revelation in an allegorical manner so that they would be applicable, not only to believers, but to those who responded to the ballet in human terms. As he said to me: "There are many symbols in the

135

carrying of a Cross." He was drawn to consider the most ancient beliefs of mankind, seen in terms of myth, where the devil exists, not so much in a theological sense, but as a presence of abiding evil both in ourselves and in modern society. "The animal is in us as well. The devil is in you, as he is in me." To balance this, "there is always hope, for people do redeem themselves and die for others and cause others to live. There is always this conflict".

He chose his dancers with this concept in his mind. He wanted three men with very strong personalities who would be able to project this darkness, this sense of evil. He needed also a girl to fulfil the role of the Madonna, and Lucy Burge, with her exceptional beauty and the poetic, lyrical quality of her dancing, was an obvious choice. The two other girls, he decided, must be small, with very fast, light movements; at that time he did not see them as cherubs which in their duet they so enchantingly became. Otherwise, beyond this vague outline of the ballet, he brought no starting images to the dancers on the first day they began work. He had all he wanted; as he put it, "there was a floor, six dancers and music. I could start from that".

In writing my account of the creation of *Black Angels*, I imagined that the opening images were already prepared in his mind, but this was not the case. "I did not even know how I was to start the choreography until I was in the studio that first morning with the dancers and the music. Then I decided that they must all fall out of heaven into hell, and so I got them to run onto the stage and do that. I remembered a movement I had thought of some considerable time earlier showing claws curling inwards, so the movement from the floor rose up into that image." Thus from each image, organically, the ballet developed in the manner I have described, yet with such expressive clarity that when Christopher Bruce read my account of the choreography as it was created, he did not feel, either in detail or as a whole, that it had been misunderstood. I say this, not to give credit to myself, but rather to stress the precision of each image as it was created, articulate even on the most profound level of human experience.

"It is a ballet about the Christian religion" (Bruce says) "but

136

it deals with universal themes." It can, he maintains, be judged on many levels, and he is content that there should be a number of different concepts contained in a single image. One of these is the use of the dancer's body to express a cross, and the manner in which this can be transformed into other images—those of wings or serpents—within a tiny phrase of the music.

One of the most beautiful and moving moments in the ballet is when Catherine Becque stands motionless, her body formed in the shape of a cross which Zoltan Imre then carries on his back on the road to Calvary. He falls, and she kneels on his prostrate body; she is lifted to hover over him like an angel, then resumes the position of a cross. Christopher Bruce describes the creation of these exquisite images in an entirely unpretentious manner, as if such a superb design in movement was a matter of practical mechanics. In a sense, as he talked, one could recognize Valéry's "cool scientist" putting into effect the ideas of the "subtle dreamer". It was so casual, so matter-of-fact: "I knew I wanted the image of Cathy on his chest, but then the problem arose how to get her off. Then I thought, 'wouldn't it be marvellous if she just hovered above him'. So we did that. Then he pressed her upwards with one hand, and it did not matter that he found this difficult to do, because it is exactly the struggle it takes to lift the Cross up and slot it into the hole in the ground."

One sees here the intensity of his visual imagination, and the way it develops so freely, one image leading into another, as if contained in potential within it. Yet all the time he is creating the ballet, Bruce is making continual adjustments to the structure, to achieve the right balance between fast and slow sections, between solos, duets and group dances, between those sections that carry greater emotional weight than others. But this is not so much planned, as felt, and is also determined by the construction of the music. "You have got to be continually aware of the structure, and aim not to lose the proportions of the work as a whole." He agrees that the solo for Lucy Burge is the peak of the work, and it still moves him profoundly. "Lucy's solo is my faith."

It was at a late stage that he decided to change the end of the

ballet, so that it concluded on a note more ambiguous, more tentative than he had first envisaged. As we have seen, there was no redemption for the black angels; the Devil still walked the world. It could not, he thought, end on the note of the triumph of good over evil as he had first envisaged. "Finally it seemed the music was just not saying that. It could not be any other way than the way it ended. You can't go against what you feel to be right. The Devil comes forwards at the end of the ballet, as a warning to us all that evil does exist, and there is no finality in its defeat."

Christopher Bruce felt he could not go further in describing his ballet. "It is" (he said) "strangely mysterious to me now. I feel it, but I cannot put it into words." And this is as it should be: if one could explain a poem, a dance, or a piece of music in terms of words you would deny its essence. A work of art is self-contained: a ballet only truly exists when it is being danced; afterwards we can search for its meaning, but that meaning, outside the dance, is, as I have said earlier, beyond our grasp or our understanding.

After completing the choreography, Christopher Bruce was not able to work on it, apart from "running it through" three or four times, until the rehearsals. During this period the dancers were learning five new ballets for their London season; it was inevitable that when they returned to *Black Angels* some of the initial inspiration had been lost, and in the early "run-throughs" the dancers were unhappy about their performances, indeed quite disconsolate. "We'll be better soon," one of them said to me rather sadly, even doubtfully, as if she did not believe it herself. But by the time they had been through the ballet for the last time before the final rehearsals, the edge had returned to their dancing; again they began to respond to the intensity and beauty of the images. Indeed, after the sudden dryness and lack of inspiration that followed upon the completion of the choreography, suddenly they found new emotions within it, a commitment to the work more total even than in the period of its making.

The first rehearsal with the musicians was held at the studio five days before the opening night. During the "run through" of the ballet, the dancers had some difficulty in adjusting to the different timbre and variations in tempo compared to the tape from which they had previously rehearsed. There were lapses in memory, so closely had they associated each movement with a particular tempo and the shape of the musical phrase, while at times the steps became blurred, curiously lacking in focus. Then other moments gained a new clarity and brilliance of outline as the music sharpened the dance, gave to it a sudden vividness, each step cut with a daring precision. Sometimes the dancers had more space musically in which to form the images; at others they seemed cramped by the music, the long flowing lines sketched here and there with an uncertain brevity.

The rehearsal would be broken while Christopher Bruce discussed matters of tempo and phrasing with the conductor, Adam Gatehouse; sometimes, also, individual dancers would complain of difficulties created for them by phrasings which varied in small details from those with which they associated their dance. These discussions were conducted with admirable good humour and a complete absence of any sign of irritation or discourtesy, in an atmosphere of generosity and mutual co-operation so typical of the Company.

At the half-way point in the ballet the rehearsal was stopped so that the choreographer could discuss details with the dancers, mostly aimed at recovering the clarity of the images, lost to a certain extent in their uncertainty and lack of confidence in the music. Twice the first devils' dance, which had caused so much trouble all during the creation of the ballet, was rehearsed in order to regain a sense of its variable dynamics, the contrast between strong and less strong movements, and the different shading of emotion from gestures expressing defeat to those indicating a kind of arrogant acceptance of their fate, a glorying in their damnation. It is in this dance that the fallen angels are first crushed by their fate, indicated by the limping dance in diagonal across the stage with which it opens, while later they accept it with a defiant sweep of their arms, the stamping of rebellious feet.

One can understand why Christopher Bruce sets so much

importance to exact precision in dynamics here, since it is at this point that the duality of the attitude of the fallen angels is first expressed, and this theme is to run through the whole ballet. Bruce asks the dancers to move at right angles across the stage, so that they face the musicians and can pick up the conductor's beat. In the second devils' dance, the same problems occur in reconciling the dance to the musical rhythm, reawakened by the slightly different tempo of the string quartet to the music on tape.

Then the rehearsal continues from this mid-point until the end of the ballet. In her wonderful solo Lucy Burge dances with a glorious sense of *plastique*, more marked now than in any of her previous attempts, where each phrase is carried through in long, flowing lines of astounding beauty; each pose opens like a flower to the light of the music. Her face is rapt—a kind of serene wonder, as if she listens to the choir of angels that sang once in a cave and to a child in a manger.

In this second half of the ballet the dancers have grown more accustomed to the music and adjust with great skill to the small changes in tempo, although the difference in texture, accentuated by the loudness of the music and its echo in such a small space, limits their emotional response. They have difficulty in picking up their cues, both technical and emotional, and one realises how closely the dance is related to the music as the dancers first hear it, so that it is absorbed by them to a depth one had not originally suspected.

At this first rehearsal with the musicians one had the sense rather of actors in a play where the cast had been changed or the lines subtly rewritten, so that they find it hard to adjust. Yet, at other moments, the response is more intense; they are caught up in the music, suddenly excited, and as the rehearsal continues these moments become more frequent, so that one catches a glimpse of the ballet as it will be performed for the first time on the stage. `

After completion of this "run through" Christopher Bruce does some further work on Lucy Burge's solo. For him this is the key point in his work, now marvellously executed by the dancer, so that he had the pleasure a writer or painter might gain in adding tiny details to a section in which he is most deeply satisfied. It is, for a writer as well (I suspect) as for a choreographer, easier to improve on the best passages than bring those that are less satisfactory up to the required standard: the first is truly creative, but the second merely technique, where the artist has not the necessary spark to fire his imagination.

Bruce also makes some small changes to the phrasing in the duet for Catherine Becque and Sylvia Yamada, now most happily referred to as "the dance of the two cherubs". Indeed these two tiny dancers look so charming in this intricate dance, that one must presume they have been driven from heaven as a result of some oversight. They belong more to the glittering air in paintings by Botticelli than to the pit of hell; like a pair of winged cherubs they blow their golden trumpets at the corner of some great canvas of Renaissance art.

There is to be another rehearsal on the following day. The dancers leave the studio, the musicians pack up their instruments and carry out the group of tuned glasses on which they play their "God-music". Almost immediately the rehearsal for the next new ballet begins.

The second days' rehearsal with musicians went far more smoothly. The dancers had grown accustomed to the variations in tempo between the string quartet and the recording, and only a few small points, notably in Lucy Burge's solo, required attention. At this rehearsal the girls wore practice clothes instead of their stage costume as on the previous day, but Zoltan Imre and Bob Smith were in costume.

It was the first hot day of summer, and one recalled how we had all arrived muffled up against the cold when the choreography was begun. Now the sweat streamed off the dancers, and in the heat the roaring of traffic from the High Road sounded louder, so that the windows had to be closed. Even though, in this one day, they had five new ballets to rehearse, the atmosphere was relaxed, as it had been on the first day when the dancers began work on *Black Angels*. If they were tired and overworked, as they must have been, they did not show it.

Christopher Bruce began the rehearsal with further work on the duet for the two cherubs, to which, with its intricate embroidery in the movements of the hands—at times in attitudes that were like whispered prayers, at others held palms-outwards, as if they patted a ball one to another—the choreographer had obviously become deeply attached. He adjusted an angle slightly, standing back to observe the effect as a woman might, setting a bowl of flowers. As they joined hands in a series of poses of extraordinary delicacy, these two bright little dancers made out of the dance a glittering chain, intricately linked by small steps and tiny gestures.

The final section of the ballet was then "marked" by all the dancers, so that they could get the feel of the music, and adjust to small changes in tempo. Bruce then returned to the second devils' dance, showing how the slightly slower tempo of the music allowed them time to fill out their movements, so that the long *arabesques* could be more widely stated to prove a greater contrast to the distortions within the choreography. Particular attention was given to the forming of the hands, the fingers twisted as if gripped by some terrible ague.

The dancers then ran through the whole ballet, dancing with a new intensity now that they felt more sure of the music, adding here and there their own tiny details to the choreography. Their response to the music was closer now than it had ever been, drawing from them an extended emotional range, evoked, seemingly unconsciously, from their personal reactions to the music. When he spoke to the dancers afterwards Christopher Bruce recognized this and welcomed it, even encouraging them to make their own personal adjustments to the choreography in a way he would not have done while he was creating the ballet. But now, in a sense, it was outside him, completed and belonging to his dancers and soon to the public, so that he had achieved a distance from it, a sense of emotional detachment. "I like to leave the choreography alone now," he said, "add no more details." Indeed he warned the dancers that the choreography must now appear less abstract to them; they must respond to it emotionally, as they feel it in their dancing.

"You should weep real tears now," Bruce says, "but you are

the damned so that they are not for others. For them you have only crocodile tears; the real ones are for yourselves." He warns the dancers to be totally involved in the work even at those moments when they are not dancing; the transitions, the walks across the stage, must be a dance full of emotion. "You must", he says "be always aware, feel your limbs scream out in every movement." The walks and poses should be "electric"; the anguish throbs in their limbs, even in moments of stillness.

The dancers are dismissed. Suddenly there is an air of finality, a curious emotional void. I feel it also, now no longer involved; to me it brings a kind of sadness, a sense almost of loss. The ballet now belongs to the dancers; it has been handed over to them so that they can create it anew each time they dance.

The day of the first performance at the Arts Centre of Christ's Hospital School, Horsham, was a long and exacting one for the dancers. From 10 a.m. until 2 p.m. they were involved in lighting rehearsals, where they had to "walk through" all the choreography, while the complex pattern of lighting cues was created by John B. Read. Although this was slow and tedious work for them, they remained in high good humour, relaxing, cat-like, at snatched moments or indulging in small jokes in movement to vary the monotony. It was cold in the theatre, and Christopher Bruce prowled between the auditorium and the stage wrapped in a thick blanket.

Continually, small adjustments were made to the lighting plan, as John Read varied his pattern, so that it seemed he painted the air very rapidly with strokes of light. At one point Christopher Bruce asked him if he could have "more fire on the arms"; later, there were a number of experiments to achieve exactly the right balance of cold blue light for Lucy Burge's solo. A number of supplementary lights had been added to the theatre's already extensive system, and John Read conveyed his technical instructions to the lighting box, where, to one's surprise, the technician was a boy from the school, whose response was exact and entirely professional.

This is the unique feature of the Arts Theatre. Not only the front of the house staff but also the stage hands and technicians are all boys from the Christ's Hospital School to whom the theatre belongs. They are highly skilled, even when extremely young, and work happily with the various professional companies of actors, dancers and musicians who perform at the Arts Theatre.

Beautifully situated near the main quadrangle of the school, the theatre has a fine stage—wider than that of Sadler's Wells Theatre—and is superbly equipped. It now attracts audiences from a radius of some twenty-five miles, as well as many visitors from London. The elegant auditorium with its red ceiling and wooden balconies, also painted in bright red trellis work, set in two tiers around the theatre, reminded me of photographs of theatres in the deep South of America. A friend told me the theatre was very similar to one she had visited in New Orleans, while my companion, Judy Ling Wong, thought it was like those she had seen in China and Malaya. Surrounded by playing fields and open land, it is both surprising and enchanting, hidden away like a bright jewel among the trees and buildings.

At 2 p.m. there were photo calls followed by a short break, with class at 3 p.m. and the dress rehearsal an hour later. The first signs of nervousness began to appear: Catherine Becque was concerned that her hair was too neatly groomed for hell, so that Nadine Baylis tied into it little strips of black nylon to give the right, unkempt look. Lucy Burge was worried that in certain poses in *arabesque* during her solo she caught her foot in the hem of her dress, so that Nadine Baylis snipped sections from it to free her limbs. Zoltan Imre lay flat on his back, eyes closed, on the comfortable rock that in the ballet was to be his tomb. His skin glowed like ivory in the light of the flames.

Seen for the first time moving in this new world of light, the dancers appeared to spring out of the music with a fierce urgency, the air around them flickering, adder-like, in the distant glow from hell's fire. Nadine Baylis' *décor* of such dark majesty rose above them on brooding wings. It seemed malignant, full of menace—a vast hanging bat, outstretched against the stars. It was also a cold cavern lit by hidden fires, the ante-room to hell. The dancers' limbs were touched with unearthly colours, shadows of green and blue and red, set against the cold pallor

of their skins, now glazed and shiny like those of the dead.

The dress rehearsal was, for me, the most moving performance of all, in this near empty theatre with a few people scattered around the stalls and a group of boys watching from the first balcony. All the images I had seen in the studio at each moment of their shaping now throbbed with new life and vivid colour, as if the lighting design were the music made visible as it flickered and blazed round those tormented limbs.

The rehearsal over, Christopher Bruce went up to the stage to give his last comments to his dancers. John B. Read again ran over all the lighting cues with his technician. The curtain calls were rehearsed; somehow now the dancers looked small and vulnerable against the vast splendour of their setting, as they bowed to the nearly empty auditorium. Then they gathered up their belongings and left the stage, in a way like a group of nomads, strolling players from centuries ago, to rest a little before their dancing began.

Epilogue

Black Angels was first danced in public at the Arts Centre, Horsham on 11th May, 1976; again performed at the Théâtre de la Ville, Paris on 18th May. It received its London *première* at Sadler's Wells Theatre on 16th June, the opening night of Ballet Rambert's jubilee season. These and subsequent performances in Britain and abroad are part of another story in which I am only involved as a member of the audience. Indeed the first night was like turning the last page of this book. My story was finished, and I felt the loss of it, even as the curtain rose.

Now the ballet no longer belongs to the small group of dedicated artists who combined to create it, for it is shared indiscriminately among a public, most of whom will be indifferent to the hours of its making. And it is right so: when a new work of art emerges into the light it should at first be something magical, sudden and full of mystery—a phoenix that springs from the heart's fire. I felt this too, even though I knew the ballet so well in every stage of its creation; it was new to me on that first night. Yet for me it was also an ending. For the dancers, each time they dance will be a new beginning, a new adventure in their restless art.

S